Co

E

LANGUAGE

**David Lambert and
The Diagram Group**

HarperCollins*Publishers*

HarperCollins Publishers
Westerhill Road, Bishopbriggs,
Glasgow G64 2QT

A Diagram book first created by Diagram Visual
Information Limited of 195 Kentish Town Road,
London NW5 8SY

First published 1996
This edition published 1999

Reprint 10 9 8 7 6 5

© Diagram Visual Information Limited 1996, 1999

Photography and Art Direction – PS5 Limited

ISBN 0 00 472307 4

Printed in Italy by Amadeus S.p.A.

Introduction

Asked how people communicate with one another, most of us would say, 'With words.' We might be surprised to learn how much we express through the unspoken language of the body and the face. As well as using conscious gestures such as the 'thumbs up' and winking to convey silent messages of approval or complicity, we subconsciously send out a stream of other gestures which convey our inner attitudes and feelings. When do we exhibit them? What do they mean? How can they be interpreted?

Containing over 260 illustrations, *Collins Gem Body Language* answers these questions and more. It is an attractive and practical introduction to the conscious and unconscious body language people use to express mood, attitude and status. A summary of the gestures, postures and expressions found in the book is included, allowing the observer to pinpoint actions seen and their meanings quickly. An explanation of the origins of body language and a brief history of its study are given. Nonverbal communication from around the world is examined and interpreted. Not only is the body language common to all cultures scrutinized, but regional varieties of gestures are illustrated, and their meanings compared and contrasted.

A clear and helpful guide, *Collins Gem Body Language* will prove invaluable to the keen observer of human nonverbal communication.

Contents

Guide to actions and their meanings

Two alphabetical lists follow, both designed to help you access the information contained in this book. The first gives body parts and items of clothing used in body language. The second lists the meanings and emotions betrayed by body language.

BODY PARTS AND BODY LANGUAGE

Ankle

cross 153
see also Foot/feet, Leg(s), Shin cross

Arm(s)

crossed/folded 135, 147–9, 164, 182
embracing someone else 52, 65, 90–1
and hand waving 113
hand hooked through someone else's 44
hugging self 166
linked 65
raising the 78, 143
embracing someone else's shoulders
    44, 63
see also Hand(s), Wrist(s)

stroking a 103, 104
touching cheek 64

Chest
palms placed together in front of 85
tapping the 124
touching above heart 173

Chin
flicking 112
hand held below 123
stroking 108
tapping under 124

Ear(s)
pulling lobe of 184
rubbing the 184

Elbow
patting with hand 132
striking with hand 140

Eye(s)
blinking 106
closing the 165
contracted pupils of 119
dilated pupils of 75, 106
narrowed 31
opened wide 77
rolling the 133

Finger(s)

beating with the 37; *see also* wagging
cheek resting on 107
cheek screwed into by 104
circling temple(s) 139
crossing the 155
disguised insult with 181
drumming the 126
fiddling with an object 71, 162
fidgeting with an object 121
finger pointed at by 137
forehead tapped by 133, 138
jabbing with 37
picking at fluff 135
palm of other hand pointed at by 129
spread apart 40
stroking the throat 129
temple(s) pointed at by 160
temple(s) tapped by 133, 138
throat 'cut' by 159
twirling imaginary moustache 105
V sign made with 101, 141
wagging 113–14
see also Finger(s) and thumb(s), Fist(s),
    Hand(s), Palm(s), Thumb(s)

Finger(s) and thumb(s)

curling inwards 36

Fingernail

Fingertips

Fist(s)

Foot/feet

Forehead

Hair
flicked back 69
ruffled 62
smoothed with hand 69, 74

Hand(s)
and arm waving 92–3, 113
on another person's back 63, 146
on a cheek 107
chopping body with 161
chopping with 38, 39
clap on back 90
clasped behind back 182
cupped 93
grip, power 35–8
grip, precision 33, 34
grooming gestures made with 75
on heart 173
head placed in 166
held behind back 182
held below chin 123
held out and apart 40
holding with another person 53, 65
hooked through someone else's arm 44
in pockets 161, 182
kissing 88
on hips 76, 142
open, raised to forehead 157–8

Head

Hips

Knees

Leg(s)

Lips

Mouth

and wrists, showing the 69
see also Finger(s), Fist(s), Hand(s),
    Thumb(s)

Shin

cross 151–2
see also Ankle cross, Foot/feet, Leg(s)

Shoulder(s)

brushing specks off 75
embracing another person's 44, 63
hunching 117
looking over 68
raising one 180
shrugging 116

Temple(s)

forefinger circling the 138
forefinger pointing at the 160
forefinger(s) tapping the 133, 138

Thigh(s)

slapping the 127
stroking the 71

Throat

finger dragged across 159
grasping the 160
sawing action across the 125
stroking the 129
see also Neck

EMOTIONS AND MEANINGS

1. Discovering body language

WHAT IS BODY LANGUAGE?

Body language (or nonverbal communication) is the means by which humans (and some other animals) convey information through conscious or subconscious gestures, bodily movements or facial expressions.

Body language seems to have three broad uses: as a conscious replacement for speech; to reinforce speech; and as a mirror or betrayer of mood.

USING BODY LANGUAGE INSTEAD OF SPEECH
Nonverbal equivalents of spoken phrases include silent messages of complicity (for example, winking), insults (such as the British V sign, see p. 141) and approval (for instance, the thumbs up, see p. 99).

USING BODY LANGUAGE TO REINFORCE SPEECH
Very often hand gestures are used subconsciously by speakers to reinforce the points that they are making vocally. The signals also reflect their desire that what they are saying should be accepted by their listeners (see pp. 33–42).

BODY LANGUAGE AS A REFLECTION OF MOOD
Some nonverbal signals, such as a happy smile or an angry scowl, are often consciously produced and easily spotted and interpreted. Others – for example, body pointing and dilated eye pupils (see p. 106) – are not conscious signals

of mood. Rather, they tend to betray an inner feeling or attitude that the person who signals them is unaware of or wants to conceal. Such signals can be easily missed or misidentified unless seen in their social context or as part of a 'gesture cluster' involving other parts of the body.

EARLY PROGRESS

Body language is as old as our species, but scientific understanding of it dates mainly from the last few decades, when social psychologists and anthropologists working mostly in the United States began making detailed analyses of its components. There were a few, however, who made studies before the twentieth century.

THE 1600S
The first book on body language appeared more than 350 years ago. John Bulwer's *Chirologia: or the Naturall Language of the Hand* (1644) was a pioneering survey of meaningful hand movements.

THE 1800S
Nineteenth-century teachers of drama and pantomime showed how actors could convey feelings through facial expression and body movement.

1900
Wilhelm Wundt, the German founder of experimental psychology, published Volume 1 of his *Volkerpsychologie* ('Ethnic Psychology'), with an important theoretical chapter on the language of gestures.

BODY LANGUAGE AND ANIMAL BEHAVIOUR

THE 1800S

An early landmark in the scientific study of nonverbal communication was the naturalist Charles Darwin's *The Expression of the Emotions in Man and Animals* (1872). This influential work was the first to claim that humans, apes and monkeys express certain emotions by similar facial expressions inherited from a common ancestor. Darwin's work inspired research which led to the science of ethology: the study of animal behaviour.

THE 1900S

In 1969, British zoologist Desmond Morris created a popular publishing sensation by giving an ethological interpretation of human actions in his best seller *The Naked Ape*. In *Manwatching* and later books and television programmes, Morris again showed how much we owe nonverbal communication to our animal nature.

KINESICS AND PROXEMICS

Kinesics and proxemics form the basis of the modern study of nonverbal communication.

KINESICS

Kinesics is the study of communication by the bodily movements used when people talk to one another.

PIONEERS IN KINESIC STUDIES

Ray L. Birdwhistell, an American anthropologist, pioneered kinesics. He analysed people's actions by using slow-motion replays of films showing conversations. He published his findings in books including *Introduction to Kinesics* (1952).

Albert E. Scheflen, an American psychiatrist, also helped pioneer kinesics. He argued that human activity consists of small, regular actions grouped into larger ones. He found that courtship followed a predictable sequence of actions. He also noticed that people assume different postures when including or excluding others in a group, and that individuals' postures changed to mirror those of people they agreed with.

Gerhard Nielsen of the University of Copenhagen found that a young American male and his partner followed a 24-stage sequence of actions from his first approach to sexual intercourse.

Edward H. Hess showed that seeing an attractive person or object makes the pupils of the eyes expand.

Paul Ekman, an American researcher, with colleagues Friesen and Wallblatt in 1980, coined several terms for use in kinesics research. These terms are 'emblem' (a symbolic hand movement with a verbal meaning known to a particular group; for example, the thumbs up, see p. 99), 'illustrator' (a hand movement emphasizing speech rhythm; for example, jabbing, see p. 37), and 'manipulator' (a self-reassuring hand movement or one performing an instrumental task; for example, straightening a tie, see pp. 75 and 162).

PROXEMICS
Proxemics is the study of how people use the space around them to convey information nonverbally.

PIONEERS IN PROXEMIC STUDIES
Edward T. Hall, an American anthropologist, invented the word 'proxemics' in the early 1960s. He discovered that

the amount of personal space people feel they need depends upon their social situation.

Robert Sommer, an American psychologist, used the term 'personal space' in 1969. It means the 'comfortable separation zone' that people like to keep around them. He listed the uneasy reactions of hospital patients when he intruded upon their personal space.

CULTURE AND GENDER

The majority of the body language described in *Collins Gem Body Language* is from the Western and Islamic worlds. Research on body language from other parts of the world is less readily available. Even so, a number of African, Asian and Latin American examples have been included.

GENDER- AND CULTURALLY-SPECIFIC BODY LANGUAGE
Often the reader will notice that certain gestures tend to be performed by (or used to comment about) a specific sex or cultural group. The intention is not to be sexist or ethnically biased but, rather, to reflect gestures that are used by real people in the real world.

VARIATIONS AND INTERPRETATION

The repertoire of gestures in this book, though extensive, is not exhaustive, so variations of certain signals or gestures familiar to some readers may not have been included. The same may be said for the interpretations given. The meanings attributed to certain actions can vary from culture to culture and from region to region.

2. Expressions and gestures

Here, basic facial expressions and hand actions and their meanings are examined. There follows a checklist of most body parts, large and small, expressing body language. The chapter ends by showing that many of the actions we perform are done automatically, so that we are unaware of exactly what we do.

UNIVERSAL FACIAL EXPRESSIONS

There are at least six facial expressions found throughout the world, which would suggest that they are inborn rather than learned. They are happiness, sadness, surprise, fear, anger and disgust.

Each expression requires a combination and an amazingly subtle rearrangement of features to send a unique and immediately recognizable signal. The three independently mobile parts of the face, involved are: the forehead and eyebrows; the eyes, eyelids and upper part or 'root' of the nose; and the lower face, comprising the rest of the nose, the cheeks, mouth and chin.

Note: The expressions described below are those that might accompany very strong rather than subtle degrees of feeling.

HAPPINESS
Although it is not an exclusive signal of happiness, a smile is the most obvious sign of this feeling. Smiling chiefly affects your eyes and lower face.

1 Eyes The lower eyelids become slightly raised, with wrinkles appearing below them. Crow's feet may crinkle the skin at the outside corners of your eyes.

2 Mouth Your mouth lengthens as the corners of your lips move out and up. Your lips may part enough to show (usually your upper) teeth. A strong smile also creates a pair of wrinkles that run from outside the corners of your lips up to your nose.

3 Cheeks Your cheeks rise and bulge, perhaps high enough to make your eyes narrower, and to emphasize the mouth-to-nose and crow's feet wrinkles.

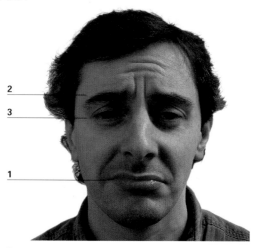

SADNESS

1 Mouth Sadness is generally betrayed by the mouth which tends to droop at the corners, so emphasizing the generally slack and unanimated appearance of the face. The lips may quiver if you are on the verge of tears.

2 Eyebrows and forehead The inner ends of the eyebrows may rise, so that the space between them, the 'root' of the nose and the eyes takes on a triangular shape. There may be slight wrinkles in the middle of your forehead above this triangular shape.

3 Eyes These might glisten with unshed tears.

SURPRISE
1 Forehead and eyebrows When you are startled, your
eyebrows curve and shoot upwards, and wrinkles
corrugate your forehead right across its breadth.
2 Eyes The whites of your eyes are displayed as you open
your eyes wide.
3 Mouth Your jaw drops, opening your mouth slackly.

FEAR
When you are scared, parts of your face react much as they do in surprise. In most parts of the world, however, there are subtle differences.

1 Eyebrows and forehead Your eyebrows rise and are pulled together. They appear to be somewhat less curved than in a surprised expression. Once more wrinkles furrow your forehead, but this time not right across its breadth.
2 Eyes Your upper eyelids rise, exposing the whites of your eyes; your lower eyelids tense and rise too.
3 Mouth Your lips may be tensely pulled back around your open mouth.

ANGER
1 Eyebrows When you feel angry, muscles pull your
eyebrows down and inward, and vertical wrinkles crease
the skin between them.
2 Eyes These narrow as your upper and lower eyelids
move closer together. Your eyes take on a hard, staring
look and they might even seem to protrude.
3 Mouth Your lips are likely to be tightly closed and
straight, and turned down at the corners, or tautly open as
if fixed in a shout.
4 Nose Some enraged people flare their nostrils.

DISGUST
When something disgusts you, the feeling is reflected
mainly in your eyes and the lower part of your face.

1 Eyes Your lower eyelids rise and lines appear in the skin
below them.
2 Mouth, nose and cheeks You wrinkle your nose and
your cheeks move up. You might raise both lips, or just
your upper lip, lowering your lower lip and making a
slight pout.

HAND GESTURES

Apart from the face, the most visually expressive features
are the hands. Hands are so important to us that we

mobilize them even when they have no useful work to do. Forming special shapes with their hands, speakers beat them to and fro like a conductor's baton in time to their words, unconsciously reinforcing their meaning by mimicking the actions or situations which their words convey. Some actions are based upon the precision and power grips – the two basic ways we have of grasping objects. Gesticulations also mimic hitting, cutting, begging and other actions. Here are a selection of beating signals, identified by Dr Desmond Morris, that speakers use for different kinds of emphasis.

PRECISION GRIPS
When we hold small things (such as pens or needles) between our thumb and fingertips, we are using a precision grip. It enables us to manipulate objects precisely. During speech, we might display empty-handed precision grips when we want to make a point with great nicety. They are made with the palm of the hand facing the body.

1 Thumb touching index finger
A speaker using this gesture mimics the precise grip of a craftsman manipulating a fine tool. The speaker seems to be reinforcing a statement made with precision and delicacy (see also 'Signing OK', pp. 100–1).

2 Thumb touching fingers

This can also indicate that the speaker wants to make a point with precision and delicacy (but see p. 128 for an alternative meaning).

3 Thumb almost touching index finger

In this action, the thumb and finger don't quite meet. The speaker may perform it while asking a question or when feeling uncertain about a point at issue.

POWER GRIPS

We use a power grip when we need to wield an object, such as a hammer, with force or when we need to grasp something (like a handrail or strap) to steady ourselves in a moving train, for example. The whole hand is employed; the object is held against the palm, with the fingers and thumb securely curled around it. While speaking, we tend to display this grip, empty-handed, in either a mild (hand bent) or a forceful (closed fist) form. The grips mostly show a speaker's wish to make a point with strength or to control the audience. They, like precision grips, mostly tend to be made with the palm of the hand facing the body.

1 Fingers and thumb make a tightly closed fist
This is a forceful power grip and it often signals conviction and determination, and is known to and can deliberately be exploited by public speakers and politicians who might, in reality, have neither.

2 Fingers and thumb curl inwards as if loosely grasping an object
This is a mild power grip and is usually employed by a person saying something without great force or conviction, but who nevertheless wishes to be taken seriously.

3 Fingers and thumb curve as if almost but not quite grasping an invisible object
The speaker may be trying to establish authority over an audience.

SYMBOLIC BLOWS

During speech we may use a hand like a weapon delivering a blow of some kind, whether a jab, a punch or a chop. The blows are delivered in empty air rather than on an object. The palm of the hand or the fingers tend to face outward. When we use these, we are betraying a forcefulness of feeling and an unwillingness to be contradicted.

1 Jabbing

A speaker who is verbally attacking an individual rhythmically jabs a forefinger at the person as if stabbing him or her.

2 Beating

A domineering speaker raises a forefinger and beats it up and down in an action that is symbolic of a stick (or an ape's overarm blows) pummelling an opponent into submission.

3 Punching
The speaker beats the air with a tightly clenched fist, or both fists, to lend force to an aggressive statement.

4 Chopping
A forceful speaker may underline his or her determination to cut through obstacles by making downward chopping motions with a hand forming a shape symbolic of an axe blade.

5 Scissoring or double-chopping

In this gesture the forceful speaker crosses both forearms and makes outward cutting motions with both hands. The speaker might be using this gesture while verbally rejecting a whole clutch of policies or beliefs with which he or she disagrees.

6 Handing-off

The speaker holds up one hand or both hands, open and palm forward as if to fend off someone's hostile approach. This might accompany verbally rejecting an idea.

OPEN-HAND GESTURES

Apart from chopping and handing-off gestures (see pp. 38–9), open-hand gestures mostly show a speaker's wish for rapport with an audience.

1 The 'fish measure'
The speaker holds out both hands side by side, as if indicating the size of a fish he or she might have caught, but then beats them up and down. This signals the speaker's wish to project thoughts into the listeners' minds.

2 Spreading the fingers
The speaker holds out a hand with fingers spread stiffly apart, as if wishing to make contact with everyone in an audience.

3 Palms up

The speaker extends both hands palm upwards towards the audience. People subconsciously recognize this beggar's gesture as a plea for agreement or support.

4 Palms down

The speaker holds out both hands palm down and beats them up and down, a signal aimed at calming a tense situation or quietening a noisy audience so the speaker can go on talking.

5 Palms in

The speaker holds both hands in front with palms facing the body, as if encircling someone. This gesture can stress the speaker's efforts to bring the audience closer to his or her way of thinking. It can also indicate the speaker's own attempts to grasp a proposition or hypothesis.

3. Keeping your distance

Like many animals, humans claim, mark and defend areas against other individuals of their own species.

THE THREE ZONES OF DEFENCE

The area most animals defend can be divided into three zones: the zone immediately around the body; the nest where the animal raises its young; and the feeding ground or territory within the home range roamed by the animal as it searches for food or a mate.

For humans, these three areas broadly correspond to personal space, the home and (if there is one) the garden. Our concerns here, however, are with the ways in which gesture and posture betray someone's proprietorial feelings (warning-off signals) for an object or person; and with personal space, its maintenance and the individual's adjustment to its loss.

PERSONAL TERRITORY

FIGHTING FOR TERRITORY

On their own ground, animals become much braver and more aggressive than outside it. They show hostility to any intruder and may fight to drive it out. Even if the intruder is more powerful, the territory holder tends to fight with more determination and confidence, and usually wins.

Humans, too, feel more dominant on their home ground than outside it. Accordingly, a stranger invited into someone's house or a soccer supporter at an away match might well feel at a disadvantage.

WARNING OTHERS OFF

Constant territorial fights would make life impossible. Many animals avoid fighting by following generally accepted codes of behaviour. A bird sings to proclaim its control over a clump of trees. A mammal may mark its territory's boundaries with urine, faeces or scent from a special scent gland. Most potential intruders recognize these sounds and scents as 'keep out' signals and obey them. If they do stray over an invisible boundary, instead of immediately attacking, the resident might perform a ritualized threat display which scares them away before any blood is shed.

So it is with humans. We add personal touches to our homes and other possessions to show that they are ours. Other people then keep off. If we invite them in, we behave in subtly dominant ways (see pp. 145–6) and they feel constrained to behave less freely than they would in their own homes. Burglaries and aggressive invasions of privacy are the exceptions to these everyday rules.

SHOWING OWNERSHIP

We use postures and gestures to show that we lay claim to someone or something that we consider our personal territory. Some common examples of proprietorial postures and gestures are given below.

- A wife who wants to make her relationship to her husband clear to onlookers might hook her hand through his arm as they go for a stroll (**1**). A husband might show 'ownership' of his wife in a public place by putting an arm around her shoulders.

- Someone posing for a photograph with his or her new car, of which he or she is eager to show ownership, might place a hand on its roof or a foot on its bumper.

- A householder talking to someone at the door is likely to lean on the doorpost in a proprietorial way (**2**).

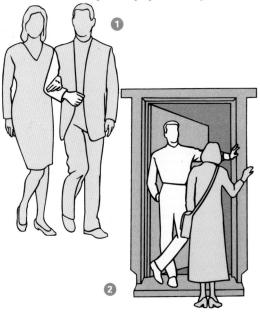

- A business executive might signal ownership of, and ease in, a work space by sitting with a leg across the arm of an office chair, or by resting both feet on the office desk (**3**) or on an open desk drawer.

PERSONAL SPATIAL ZONES

As well as making our ownership of things or people clear to others, we are also jealous of the space that immediately encircles us. We each try to maintain an invisible space bubble or spatial zone around us.

On neutral ground, most individuals respect each other's personal zones, and take care to keep outside them, even though we are sociable creatures.

THE FIVE SPATIAL ZONES

Students of human behaviour have identified five concentric spatial zones affecting behaviour: the close intimate, intimate, personal, social and public zones. The zonal extents given here reflect studies carried out in mainly urban English-speaking parts of the world.

1 close intimate zone
2 intimate zone
3 personal zone
4 social zone
5 public zone

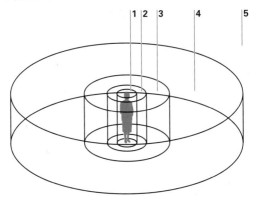

1 Close intimate zone (0–15 cm/ 0–6 in) Normally, an individual expects only a lover or a close friend or relative to come this near, and then only because they are about to touch or embrace him or her. If someone an individual doesn't like or doesn't know very well invades the intimate zone, the person's emotional reactions might be intensified forms of those described below.

2 Intimate zone (15–45 cm/ 6 in–1 ft 6 in) An individual willingly lets a lover or a close friend or relative come this near. But keeping this space clear of strangers is usually crucial to a person's feeling of comfort and security. If someone he or she doesn't know well or doesn't like moves inside the personal zone, he or she may feel stressed. The body might automatically undergo changes readying itself to cope with an unwanted sexual encounter or a physical attack.

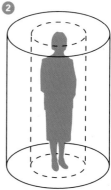

**3 Personal zone (46 cm–
1.2 m /1 ft 6 in–4 ft)** This
is how far apart most
Western people like to
stand when chatting to one
another at an office party or
some other social event (**a**).
Standing any closer would
seem unduly intimate
between new acquaintances
(**b**), yet standing any farther

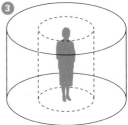

apart would also seem wrong (**c**). For while an individual
might subconsciously feel threatened if someone stands
too close to him or her, the person could also feel rebuffed
if they stand too far away. This reflects human nature as
competitive yet sociable.

4 Social zone (1.2–3.6 m/4–12 ft) Despite its name, this zone is farther out from the body than the personal zone used between people chatting at a party. The social zone can be seen operating in shops, in the street or at home, when customers or clients talk to shop assistants or tradespeople. The social zone seems to be adopted when some kind of business-based interaction is taking place.

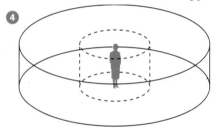

5 Public zone (3.6 m+/12 ft+) If a person is making a speech to a sizable audience, he or she tends to stand at least this far away from the front row.

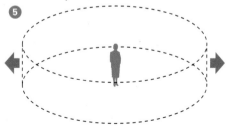

CULTURAL DIFFERENCES

How much personal space we need also varies with the part of the world in which we were raised. People from different cultural backgrounds tend to stand at different distances from each other when they talk. Some examples of these differences are given below.

- When two North Americans or West Europeans talk one could touch the other with the fingertips of an outstretched arm.
- When two Russians talk one could touch the other with the wrist of an outstretched arm.
- When two Latin Americans, Italians or Arabs talk one could touch the other with an elbow.
- People from English-speaking countries, Japan and northern Europe tend to avoid casual touching.
- People from China, France, India and Ireland generally accept some casual touching.
- People from Latin America, the Mediterranean, the Middle East, Russia and parts of Asia tend to freely practise casual touching.

ZONAL CULTURE SHOCKS
When people from two cultures meet, their different spatial needs and assumptions can cause some embarrassment, as some of these examples of possible situations show.

Chatting distances At international gatherings of academics, businessmen or diplomats, awkward situations can arise when someone from a 'wrist-length' culture holds a conversation with a person from an 'arm-length' culture. If the closer-contact individual moves nearer, the other person might feel threatened and draw back to preserve his or her personal space from invasion. This 'invasion' and 'retreat' could go on until the retreating individual is prevented from moving back further by a wall or other obstacle, or until the interaction comes to an end.

Greetings
A Latin American might greet a foreign business colleague with a hug, to that person's confusion if he or she comes from North America (**1**).

Friendly intentions
A European businessman visiting an Arab country might be alarmed if a new and friendly Arab business acquaintance chooses to take his hand as they walk down a road (**2**).

Shaking hands
A Korean businessperson, schooled to avoid touching or eye contact, would probably feel uncomfortable if his or her Western counterpart were to shake the Korean firmly by the hand and look him or her straight in the eye (**3**).

MAINTAINING PERSONAL SPACE

Whenever people begin to collect in a group, they
generally have to adjust their ideas of how much space
they need to conserve around them as newcomers crowd
in. Notice how this process influences human behaviour in
everyday situations such as those given below.

1 At a hairdresser's A hairdresser's has a row of chairs for
waiting customers. If the first customer sits at one end of

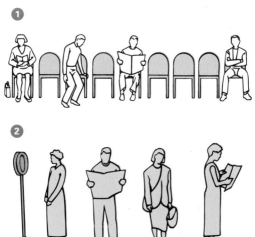

the row, the next customer is likely to sit half way along. That way, the second person feels neither uncomfortably close to the first, nor far enough away to feel isolated and appear 'stand-offish'. If a third customer sits at the other end, a fourth will probably sit half-way between the middle customer and one of those at the ends. As more people come in, the gaps between customers go on shrinking until some are forced to sit next to each other. Similar behaviour tends to occur in a doctor's waiting room, a cinema, a bus or a train.

2 In a queue People stand as if in invisible space bubbles separating them from those in front and behind. If a queue is observed from one side, everyone tends to be spaced much the same distance apart. If space is limited, the space bubbles shrink.

ADJUSTING TO LOST PERSONAL SPACE

Sometimes it is impossible to keep space bubbles intact. In a crowded lift, escalator, bus or underground train, people sit or stand so close together that their bodies are often touching. Normally, if strangers came this close to an individual, he or she would feel stressed enough for the body to undergo physiological changes readying it for fight or flight (see 'Intimate zone', p. 48).

THE ART OF IGNORING OTHERS

The adjustment to crowded conditions is different, however: everyone ignores each other. People reduce others to 'non-persons' by blocking the transmission of their own social signals. Some techniques used to achieve this are given below.

- The individual tends to stand or sit still. The larger the crowd, the less the person moves any part of the body.

- The individual generally becomes poker faced. The blank expressionless faces of rush-hour commuters usually mean they are trying not to communicate, not that they feel as miserable as they appear to be.

- Standing packed shoulder to shoulder, people tend to avoid looking at their neighbours and stare at the floor or ceiling instead.

- If there is room to hold a book or newspaper, an individual holding one might appear to find it intensely absorbing.

WHEN TOUCHING OTHERS IS UNAVOIDABLE

Even in crowds when people sometimes cannot avoid touching each other, they try to let only the shoulders and upper arms come into contact. If, however, more intimate contact is made, they might try to move apart, though the effort seems futile.

4. Getting together

We lower at least some of the invisible barriers around us for people we know and like. The closer a relationship becomes, the farther we move inside each other's defensive zones. In order to build a relationship (other than a family one), we must first get acquainted. Even before we become acquainted, we usually (not always) form first impressions. The first time we see someone – say at a workplace or party – we are likely to make a snap decision about the kind of person he or she is, and whether or not we shall like him or her.

FIRST IMPRESSIONS

Our earliest impression is based chiefly on outward appearance: partly clothes and hairstyle but mainly on face and body. Of course, once we have got to know someone as an individual, we might find that our original opinion was wrong. People we thought unattractive can seem more appealing if we discover that they share our own interests, while people we find physically attractive sometimes turn out to be rather less interesting or likeable than we initially believed.

GETTING ACQUAINTED

Once we see someone whose general appearance we like, we tend to make contact. Several signs generally seem to be displayed by two people of the same or opposite sex who are in the process of getting to know one another at a social gathering.

FRIENDLY INTEREST

This might be signalled as outlined below.

- One person looks across a room and catches another's eye.
- They approach each other, shake hands and introduce themselves.
- They might stand, half-facing each other, personal-zone distance apart (see p. 49).
- As they talk, they smile at each other a lot.
- Each pays close attention to what the other is saying.
- The listener keeps nodding to encourage the talker.
- As they talk, they may start to feel more at ease with each other and show it by changing their postures and gestures (see pp. 167–9).
- As the feeling of ease or agreement increases, they might even start to mimic each other's attitudes unconsciously (see pp. 97–8).

SEXUAL INTEREST

When two strangers some distance apart are sexually attracted to one another, they might betray this by glancing between each other's eyes and crotch. According to some researchers, this behaviour is not determined by gender.

EYE CONTACT IN CONVERSATION

Eyes play an important part in all kinds of relationships. To build a relationship requires getting to know someone. Getting to know someone involves conversing. For conversation of a friendly, non-threatening variety, both participants tend to encourage one another by glancing at and away from each other. To be stared at solidly is often found to be threatening, so in friendly encounters, eye contact usually occurs in a give-and-take sequence.

Speaker's eye contact Generally, in an ordinary social encounter, the speaker glances at the listener when he or she wants:

- to start to speak;
- to check the effect of the comments made upon the listener; and/or
- a response from the listener.

The speaker tends to look away, while the thoughts and comments are flowing freely, so preventing interruption by the listener.

Listener's eye contact In most parts of the Western world, the listener tends to do more looking and watching than the speaker. According to some researchers, the amount of time the listener spends looking may vary between 30 and 70 per cent of the time. This tends to depend on the listener's cultural background and the amount of interest he or she has in the speaker. In some non-Western cultures and parts of the Western world, the speaker tends to do more looking than the listener. Once the listener takes over as speaker, the gaze behaviour usually changes to suit the new roles.

Prolonged eye contact This can occur when there is a heightening of feeling or interest between the people talking. Feelings of sexual interest, defensiveness, hostility and aggression may result in prolonged eye contact.

CONVERSATIONAL GAZING

Exactly where people look when they talk to each other gives clues to the kind of relationship they have, as the examples below show.

- During a normal, friendly conversation each person's eyes generally focus on the part of the other individual's face between the mouth and eyes (**1**).

- An experienced negotiator might give a conversation a purposeful air by focusing on the other person's forehead and eyes (**2**).

- In an intimate conversation between potential sexual partners who are at close quarters, gaze may range from eye level down to chest level (**3**).

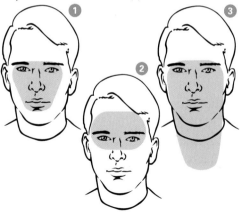

BODY CONTACTS

This is a brief guide to common types of sexual and non-sexual body contact in the West, with the likely relationships and situations involved. It is not exhaustive, and in the real world the relationship patterns might be different to those described here.

NON-SEXUAL BODY CONTACTS	
Contact	**Participants/meaning**
• One person patting another	A parent with a child, or one adult patronizing or emotionally supporting another
• One person ruffling another's hair	A father teasing a son, or one male friend teasing another
• Pulling punches	A father teasing a son or one male friend teasing another

NON-SEXUAL BODY CONTACTS (continued)

Contact	Participants/meaning
• Someone walking with a hand on a companion's back	A parent with a child or a host with a guest
• Two people handshaking formally	New acquaintances meeting
• Two people shaking hands warmly, perhaps with one person using both hands to clasp the other's right hand (**1**), or using the left hand to clasp the other's forearm (**2**) or shoulder	Close friends meeting after an absence; common everyday greeting among males in parts of Europe
• Two men embracing each other's shoulders	Two close friends meeting after an absence
• One person kissing another's cheek	Friends or relatives meeting or parting

SEXUAL BODY CONTACTS

Contact	Participants/meaning
• One person stroking another's body	A couple in an emotional world of their own
• Two people sitting cheek to cheek or standing with forehead touching forehead (**3**)	A couple in an emotional world of their own
• Two people walking embracing each other's waists	A closely bonded couple
• Two people kissing each other on the lips, open mouthed	A passionate couple

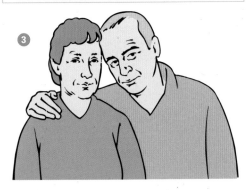

3

NON-SEXUAL AND SEXUAL BODY CONTACTS

Contact	Participants/meaning
• One person pressing an open hand against another's head (**4**)	A parent and child or lovers
• Two people walking hand in hand	A parent and child or lovers
• Two people walking with linked arms	A couple (if bodies are close together), an infirm person being supported by a friend, relative or helper (if bodies are kept apart), or female friends
• Two people flinging their arms around each other	Lovers, close relatives at a highly emotional occasion, close female friends meeting after a long absence or soccer players after one has scored a goal

NON-SEXUAL AND SEXUAL BODY CONTACTS (cont.)

Contact	Participants/meaning
• Two people kissing each other lightly on the lips	A couple not yet closely attached, or an established couple meeting or parting
• Two people sitting side by side, apparently ignoring each other (5)	Strangers (if there is a gap between them) or a well-established couple (if their bodies are touching)

COURTSHIP

A woman or man wanting to attract someone of the opposite sex sends out distinct body signals. In his book, *Body Language*, Allan Pease declares that success with the opposite sex depends upon how well individuals transmit these messages and interpret those being returned. The consensus among researchers appears to be that women display more courting signals than men.

FEMALE COURTING SIGNALS

Women give off subtler courtship signals than men and are sharper at spotting those made by the opposite sex. A woman seeing a man she finds attractive across a room might act in the ways outlined overleaf. The observations and interpretations given on the following pages are those of Allan Pease and zoologist and 'man watcher' Dr Desmond Morris.

Note: Certain body language may be exhibited for reasons other than sexual attraction. For example, a certain posture or attitude may be struck out of habit, for the sake of comfort or because of nervousness. Possible alternative interpretations are given in parentheses.

COURTING SIGNALS

The woman might:	Meaning/intention signalled
• Catch the man's eye and glance quickly away	Interest; found alluring by men because they feel the signal is a sign of hidden admiration (dislike; nervousness)
• Look at the man over a raised shoulder for longer than people normally look at each other (1)	Self-mimicry; the shoulder resembles the breast and so is sexually inviting; the long gaze signals interest

COURTING SIGNALS (continued)

The woman might:	Meaning/intention signalled
• Toss her head to flick her hair back	Interest; hair is removed from face to leave it exposed for male admiration (nervousness; habit)
• Pat and smooth her hair	Preening gesture that signals attraction to the man (nervousness; habit)
• Moisten her lips	Self-mimicry; unconsciously imitating appearance of sexually stimulated and receptive female genitals (comfort: lips need moistening; habit)
• Show the man the soft- skinned palms of her hands and insides of wrists (**2**, overleaf)	Invitation to man to caress her; wrists are considered an erogenous zone (habitual action)
• Stand with one thumb in her belt	Normally a male aggression or superiority gesture, this action aims to draw attention to the crotch (habitual stance)

COURTING SIGNALS (continued)

The woman might:	Meaning/intention signalled
• Fiddle with a cylindrical object such as a pencil, a cigarette or a wine-glass stem.	Wish to caress the man (nervousness)
• Roll her hips when she walks	Highlights the hips; draws attention to genital area (habitual gait)
• Stand or sit with legs apart	Sexual excitement; draws attention to genital area (habitual stance or posture; may be feeling superior, aggressive or impatient)
• Sit with one leg tucked under the other so that the knee points at the man and he can see the inside of her thigh; her head and body are turned towards him (3)	Sexual excitement; draws attention to genital area; body-, head- and knee-pointing in man's direction all signal interest in him (habitual posture; posture adopted for comfort)
• Sit stroking her thighs as she slowly crosses and uncrosses her legs	Wish to be caressed by the man; draws attention to genital area (comfort; altering her position)

COURTING SIGNALS (continued)

The woman might:	Meaning/intention signalled
• While sitting, twine one leg around the other (**4**)	Sexual invitation; action gives appearance of high muscle tone, which the body displays when it is ready for sexual intercourse (nervousness; shyness; habit; defensiveness)
• Sit with legs crossed, dangling a shoe half off one foot (**5**)	Phallic mimicry, as the foot makes tiny thrusting movements with the dangling shoe (nervousness; impatience; habit)

MALE COURTING SIGNALS
According to some researchers, men are clumsy at
signalling interest in someone of the opposite sex, and
slow to pick up unspoken responses, when compared with
women. A man seeing an attractive woman across a room
might make a few of the preening and other preliminary
approaches listed below, some of which mirror those used
by women. Of course, a certain posture may be struck or
gesticulation made out of habit, nervousness and so on,
rather than sexual attraction. Possible alternative meanings
are given in brackets.

Preening gestures It is believed that these form the
majority of male courtship signals.

- Smoothing the hair
  down with a hand
  (**1**; nervousness;
  habit).

- Straightening the tie (**2**; nervousness; habit; tie might need straightening).

- Sweeping fanciful specks off a shoulder with a hand (nervousness; impatience).

- Making little grooming gestures involving the collar, shirtsleeves and so on (nervousness; impatience).

Other actions These include prolonged eye gaze and drawing attention to the crotch (possible alternative meanings are given in parentheses).

- Directing a long gaze at the woman.

- Unconsciously dilating the pupils with excitement.

- If sitting, the man turns towards the woman so that one foot points in her direction (interest may be non-sexual).

- Standing or sitting with legs apart, visually stressing his genital area (**3**, see previous page; habitual posture; possibly getting ready to leave).

- If standing, the man might face the woman with hands on hips or both thumbs in his belt (a male gesture suggestive of aggression; see p. 142), drawing attention to his crotch (**4**).

5. Meeting and parting

When we meet or leave someone, we use gestures of
greeting or farewell to show that our intentions towards
the other person are friendly. Such gestures can range from
a passionate hug to formally raising a hat. They vary from
culture to culture, and according to whether we are
meeting or parting from a stranger, a friend, a relative or a
lover. By watching how people meet and part at airports
and railway stations, an observer might be able to guess
their cultural affinities and the closeness of their
relationships (see also Chapter 3).

UNIVERSAL GREETINGS

There are certain greetings that people employ all over the
world. These include the three 'recognition signals' listed
below, and hailing, waving and handshaking.

RECOGNITION SIGNALS

Whenever two people who know each other see one
another approaching, they tend to perform a simultaneous
cluster of three gestures that signal recognition (**1**, overleaf):

- they smile (**a**);
- they tilt their heads backwards; and
- they open their eyes wide (**b**), wrinkling their foreheads
  and making their eyebrows shoot up in what is known
  as the eyebrow flash (**c**).

Like the smile, the eyebrow flash has been called an inborn
(and therefore universal) reaction, but it seems to form no
part of the greeting ritual in Japan.

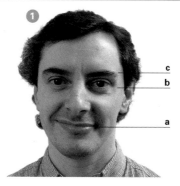

What recognition signals mean The smile signals pleasure, while the head tilt and eyebrow flash signal surprise. Put together, they say 'what a pleasant surprise it is to meet you'.

HAILING AND WAVING

Besides giving recognition signals involving the head, two people approaching each other with friendly intentions might also raise an arm in salute while they are still some way apart. Hailing or waving appears all over the world in one form or another.

Hailing Hailing is simply raising an arm (**2**) to show that you have seen the other person. Anthropologists consider that this gesture shows a friendly desire to touch someone who is still out of reach.

Waving Waving hello is often identical to waving goodbye (see pp. 92–4 for several versions).

HANDSHAKING

When two people reach touching distance, there may be some kind of body-contact display. In the Western world, two people who meet fairly formally might shake hands. As a gesture of openness showing that the hand is empty of weapons, handshaking would seem to have early origins. Some people think it goes back to the Roman practice of grasping the forearm, but handshaking as we usually do it today perhaps began only two centuries ago.

REGIONAL WAYS OF SHAKING HANDS

When two people shake hands, each usually extends the right hand with the thumb uppermost. Both hands clasp each other, palm to palm, and are pumped up and down (3). Handshaking differs in different parts of the world, as the examples below show.

- People from Northern Europe tend to pump hands up and down only once.
- People from Southern Europe and Latin America tend to pump hands up and down longer and more vigorously.

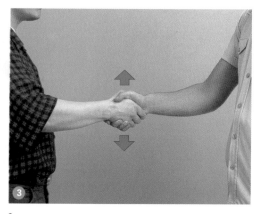

LOCAL VARIATIONS ON HANDSHAKING
Local variations on the basic handshake include some outlined opposite from the United States and Latin America, and between friends everywhere there can be special, personal ways of shaking hands.

- North American friends may greet each other by slapping the palms of the hands against each other (**4a**), then interlocking their cupped fingers (**4b**). This greeting has spread to other parts of the world.

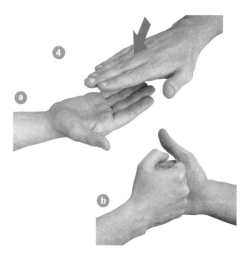

- In rural Mexico, friends might follow a handshake with each person grasping the other's thumb (**5**, overleaf).
- In many parts of the world, friends meeting after an absence might amplify their handshake with additional gestures.

THE HANDSHAKE AS A CLUE TO PERSONALITY
The firmness of a person's handshake can have different
meanings in different places. An individual who has a firm
handshake is generally thought to be sincere in the West.
In much of Asia, though, this would be a sign of an
aggressive personality.

WHO SHAKES WITH WHOM?
In most Western countries, any two people meeting for the
first time are likely to offer the right hand to be shaken,
but this is not universal.

- In parts of East Asia and North America, women and
  children seldom offer to shake hands.
- In Islamic countries, a man never offers to shake hands
  with a woman.

CULTURALLY SPECIFIC GREETINGS

Certain greetings are specific to a particular culture or
geographical region. The salaam and namaste are two such
examples.

SALAAM

The salaam is the traditional greeting used in Arabic-speaking and Islamic countries, although less widely than it once was.

Full salaam The full gesture involves sweeping the right arm upwards with the hand open and the palm facing the body (**1**).

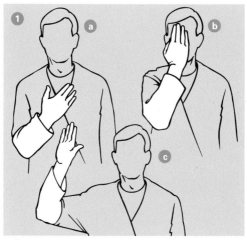

a The chest is touched above the heart.
b The hand is brought up to touch the forehead with the fingers.
c The hand then sweeps up and out.

Performed smoothly, the whole sequence looks a little like a formalized wave. As the salaam is made, the head might be nodded a little. At the same time, the traditional Arabic greeting *assalam 'alaikum* ('Peace be with you') may be uttered.

Abbreviated salaam In one abbreviated version of the salaam, the head is inclined forward, the forehead touched with the fingertips, then the hand sweeps away (**2**). Other abbreviated forms of salaam involve touching the mouth or the mouth and forehead.

Malaysian salaam This salaam involves simply extending the hands, putting the fingertips together, then placing the hands on the chest.

NAMASTE
This is the recognized gesture of greeting in India. Both hands are held up in front of the chest, palms together as if praying. At the same time, a slight bow is made (**3**). Like the handshake and salaam, namaste originated as a gesture to show that no weapons were being held.

BOWING
Bowing, once widespread in the West, now remains mostly as a specialized status display, which occurs, for example, when a European subject makes obeisance to a sovereign. Curtseying tends to be performed in much the same context. In Japan, however, it is still the traditional form of greeting used when two people meet. The general rule is

that the lower-ranking person bows first, farther, and longer, but two basic types of bow are commonly used: formal and informal.

Formal bow The body is bent forward at about 30 degrees, and the palms of the hands are placed on the knees (**4**). The action is one of bobbing up and down.

Informal bow The hands are kept at the sides and the body inclined at about 15 degrees (**5**). Both higher- and lower-ranking individuals generally bow like this when meeting informally.

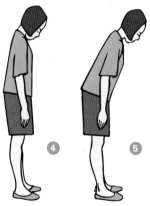

4   **5**

Easterner meeting Westerner Nowadays, a Japanese meeting someone from a Western society is quite likely to shake hands rather than bow; and handshaking, perhaps with a slight nod of the head, is the rule in Chinese society.

CLOSE-CONTACT GREETINGS

Anthropologists place bowing, handshaking, salaaming and making namaste low down on the scale of 'close-body' contacts made when two people meet.

KISSING AND NOSE RUBBING

More intimate gestures involve kissing (frowned on in much of Asia) or some other form of head contact, although even these can include fairly formal gestures.

Kissing The participants who take part in this kind of greeting, and the way in which it is performed, vary from culture to culture, as shown below.

- A person approaching or leaving a close friend or relative, might blow a kiss (**1**).

- Relatives and friends may kiss each other's cheeks (**2**; or kiss the air just short of them) on meeting and parting. In France and Russia, male friends kiss each other, though in some cultures male-to-male kissing is considered effeminate.

- A man may bow and kiss (or not quite make lip contact with) a woman's hand in a greeting suggesting old-fashioned male courtliness (**3**). This form of greeting is still common in Latin America.

Rubbing noses This traditional greeting varies greatly from culture to culture.

- Among the Inuit (Eskimos) and Sami (Lapps) of the Arctic, and in parts of Africa, Asia and the Pacific, nose tips are fleetingly pressed together or touched (**4**).

- Bedouin men touch nose-tips together three times, then smack (make a kissing sound with) their lips.

EMBRACING

All the salutations listed above can be thought of as weakened forms of embracing, a gesture involving close contact between each person's head, trunk, hands and arms. Except at moments of heightened emotion, the full embrace is less frequently seen in North America and Northern Europe than in the selected contexts illustrated below.

- In Latin America, male friends might approach one another with outstretched arms, hug and clap each other on the back (**5**).

- In Russia, male friends usually follow a firm handshake with a so-called bear hug (**6**).

- Male Polynesians meeting for the first time may embrace. After that, each man might rub the other's back.

OTHER ACTIONS PERFORMED DURING EMBRACING
Embracing in its fullest form can include certain actions, which are dependent on the relationship (see pp. 62–6)

of those involved and the emotional intensity of the
situation. These can include:

- squeezing;
- patting;
- pressing cheeks together;
- kissing;
- stroking hair;
- each person putting a hand on the other's head;
- gazing into each other's eyes;
- miling and laughing; or
- perhaps weeping.

FAREWELLS

Like greetings, partings may involve kissing and
embracing. Once a gap has opened up between people
who have just parted they may blow kisses and wave.

Waving

Waving goodbye or hello takes different forms in different
cultures. Here are several examples.

1 Sideways waving An arm and hand are held up, palm
facing forward, and the hand is waggled from side to side,
while the arm stays still. If an individual is waving to
someone in the distance, the whole arm might be waved
from side to side, or even both arms simultaneously out
and in. Sideways waving occurs all over the world.

2 The 'semaphore' wave North Americans tend to keep
the wrist stiff and 'semaphore' with the forearm and hand.
In parts of Europe, though, this would mean 'no'.

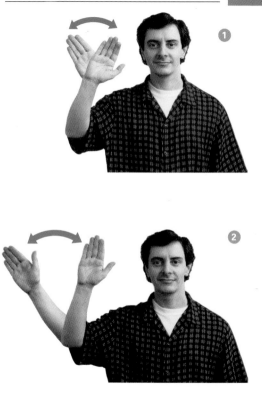

3 Patting, palm down The arm is extended with the palm of the hand facing outwards. The hand is waggled up and down as if patting the person being waved to. Waving with this kind of action is popular in certain countries, notably France.

4 Hidden-palm wave The arm is raised with the palm of the hand hidden from the other person. Again, the palm is waggled up and down.

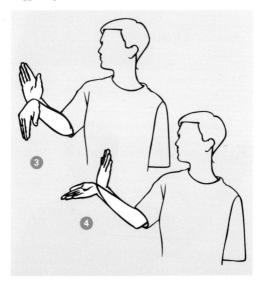

6. Being positive

When people feel positive about someone or something they often express it by an intentional gesture of agreement, reassurance, appreciation or interest. Unbidden, the body also has its own secret ways of revealing such feelings.

AGREEMENT

Instead of saying 'yes', people might make a conscious gesture that means the same thing. A 'yes' gesture can involve the head or hand.

NODDING
Most of us nod our heads up and down to signal agreement. In conversation, though, tests show that what nodding means depends on how it's done.

- A single brief nod often means 'I agree'.

- Nodding briefly now and then while someone is talking tends to show that the listener is paying attention.

- A prolonged nod could mean 'Yes, but . . .' or, in other words, 'I disagree'.

- Nodding twice in succession seems to have the effect of making the speaker change pace or return to a topic already agreed on.

- Nodding three times in succession tends to confuse the speaker, who might dry up.

SMILING
Like nodding often, giving brief, frequent smiles at someone who is talking encourages that person to continue.

Smiling is normally a positive gesture conveying welcome, happiness, agreement or appreciation, although it can also express sympathy, regret and even displeasure. The message conveyed depends upon how the smile is delivered. Research has identified nine smiles. The three main types are given here.

1 Simple smile The lips are closed, and turned up at the corners. This is how a person might smile to him- or herself.

2 Upper smile The lips are turned up at the corners and opened to expose the upper incisor teeth. This is how people usually smile at each other.

3 Broad smile The lips are turned up at the corners revealing the lower as well as the upper incisors. This smile may accompany playful laughing.

MIMICKING

Two people talking to one another might unconsciously
mimic each other's posture and gestures to show they
agree on what is being discussed. Here are some
movements that might be mimicked wherever friends
meet.

- Shifting weight from one foot to the other.
- Leaning one elbow on a drinks bar.
- Clasping a glass in both hands (**1**).
- Shifting most body weight onto one foot.
- Uncrossing the arms.
- Crossing the legs (**2**).
- Uncrossing the legs.
- Gesturing with open hands (**3**, overleaf).
- Putting a hand on your hip (**4**, overleaf).

Deliberately mimicking another person's posture and gestures can help them to feel more friendly towards the one mimicking. According to some researchers, skilful salespeople know and exploit this, but take care not to make their copying obvious. They do not move every time the potential customer moves, and when that person makes an 'openness' gesture they might signal the same message in a different way. For instance, if a seated person uncrosses the legs, instead of doing the same an experienced mimicker might gesture with both hands, palms up.

REASSURANCE

People consciously use several gestures that signal 'all's well' or 'all will be well'.

THUMBS UP

Throughout North America and Europe, raising a clenched fist with the thumb sticking up (**1**) signals 'everything's fine' (but see also p. 114). How this gesture arose is unclear. Most people believe the thumbs up sign dates from Roman gladiatorial contests when the crowd supposedly used it to signal that a fallen fighter should have his life spared. Desmond Morris, author of *Manwatching*, claims this belief stems from misreading ambiguous Latin texts and that the 'spare him' signal was really made by tucking the thumb inside the fist.

Thumbs up: alternative meanings The thumbs up sign can also mean

• a sexual insult in parts of Africa, Australia, Southern Europe and the Middle East;

• the number 1 in Germany: for example, a German might stick up a thumb to order one beer; and

• the number 5 in Japan.

SIGNING OK

Originally North American, the OK ring signal is also
found in Europe. To make it, the forearm is raised, the
tips of the thumb and first finger touching to form a ring.
The remaining fingers are extended and held slightly apart,
the hand positioned so that the fourth finger is nearest the
person being signalled to (**2**). Usually, as the hand is raised,
it is jabbed forward, as if the signaller were throwing a dart.

Signing OK: alternative meanings   The ring gesture used
for signing OK is centuries old and can also mean

• that the user thinks something is worthless (worth zero)
  in Belgium and France;

- an insult in Tunisia, Sicily and Southern Italy where the 'worthless' ring is combined with a karate chopping gesture to mean 'You are so despicable, I shall kill you'; and

- money or 'I want my change in coins' in Japan.

V FOR VICTORY

The palm faces outwards, a V is made with the first and second fingers, with the thumb and remaining fingers tucked into the palm (**3**). British premier Winston Churchill popularized this form of the V sign during World War II. In Britain, anyone wanting to signal 'we'll win' or 'peace' should make sure they do it this way, not palm inwards (which is an insult, see p. 141).

APPRECIATION

APPRECIATION OF FEMALE ATTRACTIVENESS

A whole vocabulary of gestures expresses appreciation of female attractiveness. The actions are usually made by one man to another. Some of the gestures, however, have different meanings in different places.

1 Hour-glass outline (overleaf) Using both hands to make a downward gesture tracing an hour-glass shape, representative of a woman's body, is a widespread way of saying that a woman has a lovely figure.

2 Kissing the fingertips This is a French way of praising a woman – or an exquisite dish.

3 Greek cheek stroke Gently stroking down each cheek with the thumb and first finger is a Greek way of signalling that a woman has a beautiful face.

Stroking the cheeks: alternative meanings Stroking the cheeks can

- be a sign that the person is thinking, and is prevalent in North America and other parts of the Western world;
- suggest that someone else looks ill (that their cheeks have been hollowed by illness) in Germany, Italy, the Netherlands and some other parts of Europe; and
- signal that the person has been successful in an undertaking in the former Yugoslavia.

4 Chin and beard stroking This is a way an Arab may signal that a woman has a beautiful face.

5 Rotating a first finger pressed into the cheek This is one way an Italian might praise feminine beauty.

6 Pulling the lower eyelid down This is done with a first finger and can mean 'She's an eyeful' in parts of South America. (For an alternative meaning, see p. 132.)

7 Twirling an imaginary waxed moustache This is an Italian way of showing admiration for a woman.

SHOWING INTEREST SUBCONSCIOUSLY

Most of the positive signals just described are deliberate gestures, but people exhibiting the following actions and postures may be subconsciously signalling 'I am interested'.

TELL-TALE EYES
Eyes and eyelids can give away their owner's intense interest in something or someone – perhaps a concern their owner would rather keep hidden.
Dilation of the eyes' pupils In normal lighting and conditions that are found only moderately interesting, the eyes' pupils are moderate in size (**1a**).
In dim light or if a person sees something fascinating the eyes' pupils expand (**b**). This might happen when a man sees an attractive woman, and vice versa, or when a poker player is dealt a good hand.

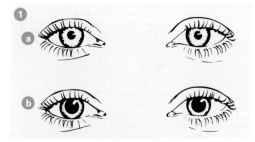

Blink rate When people see something fascinating their blink rate is likely to speed up.

HEAD ATTITUDE

The attitude of a person's head can also indicate if they are interested in what someone is saying.

Showing mild interest When an individual is neither bored nor stimulated, he or she might hold the head up (**2**).

Showing interest When a person is interested in what another is saying, his or her head tends to tilt a little to one side (**3**). He or she might also nod in agreement.

HEAD AND HAND ATTITUDES COMBINED

Head and hand attitudes combined can signal evaluation.

Interested evaluation When one person is interested in what another says and is weighing up what he or she has heard, the person might raise one hand to the cheek, first finger and thumb pointing up, and three fingers curled in on the palm (**4**).

Signs of making a decision If someone asks another to come to a decision, the second individual's hand might automatically slide down and begin to stroke the chin (**5**; see also 'Stroking the cheeks: alternative meanings', p. 103).

PROTRUDING TONGUE

Someone concentrating on making a sketch or performing some other fine work may poke the tip of the tongue out or into one side of the mouth (**6**) without even noticing what they are doing. This action is thought by some researchers to hark back to the food rejection signal of infancy. In this context, the individual's protruding tongue may signal a mild rejection to others because he or she does not want to be interrupted or distracted from the task in hand.

BODY AND LEGS
People standing or sitting in a group tend to point the torso and/or feet (and, if seated, knees or one knee) at the person who most strongly arouses their interest.

7. Being negative

Body language has dozens of ways of expressing negative
commands, feelings and inclinations. In the catch-all
sense used here, negation includes denial, ignorance,
indifference, mistrust, refusal, rejection, boredom,
sarcasm, impatience and disbelief. Besides consciously
delivered codified negatives like wagging a finger and
shaking the head, there are many subconscious cues,
warning, for instance, that an audience is losing interest
in a speaker, a party-goer is fed up with the party bore,
or a person is rejecting another's advances.
Negative signals can also be a component of other signals
such as the defensive postures described in Chapter 9.
They can combine with or lead on to others. People
feeling so negative that they want to get away adopt
'getting ready' postures, while someone in violent
disagreement might proceed to insult and aggression.

SIGNALLING 'NO'

There are more ways of signalling 'no' than might
be imagined.

HEAD SHAKING

The head is turned from side to side (**1**). This way of
saying 'no' stems from infancy, when a baby turns its head
away from from its mother's breast if it wants no more
milk. This gesture occurs worldwide, though in an
Ethiopian variant the head turns abruptly to one side only,
then faces forward again.

Head wobbling
This, confusingly, looks like head shaking but is used by Bulgarians, Indians and Pakistanis to mean 'yes'.

HEAD JERKING
The head is jerked sharply backwards (**2**). People signal 'no' like this in southern Italy, Greece, Turkey and Arabic-speaking countries. In Ethiopia, though, the same signal means 'yes'.

FLICKING THE CHIN
The head is tilted back and the chin is repeatedly flicked with the backs of the fingertips of one hand (**3**). This way of saying 'no' is common in southern Italy and neighbouring islands.

ROCKING A HAND
The hand is held up, palm outwards, and rocked quickly from side to side (**4**). The face is generally unsmiling and the head might be shaken, too. People sometimes do this to signal 'No more, thank you,' across a crowded room. An amplified version involves crossing both hands, palms outwards, in front of the chest.

WAVING
The Japanese sign 'no' by holding the right hand, turned sideways, in front of the face while waving the forearm and hand from side to side (**5**).

DON'T DO IT!

FIRST FINGER WAG
The thumb and three fingers of one hand are curled inwards, while the hand is held palm outwards and the first finger is held erect and wagged from side to side (**1**).

Wagging a first finger is a worldwide negative gesture which means 'Stop doing that'. It is often used by parents to reprimand children.

BAD NEWS

At least three popular gestures convey some form of this negative message.

THUMB DOWN

An arm is held out with thumb projecting but fingers tucked into the palm. The thumb is pointed downwards (**1**, opposite), either held still or jabbed down repeatedly. The thumb-down sign means 'bad news' or 'no good' (for the positive 'thumbs up', see p. 99). This worldwide gesture originated in Roman gladiatorial contests. The watching audience turned their thumbs down when they wanted the victor to kill the fighter he had just defeated. Turning the thumb down represented plunging a sword into the loser's body.

HOLDING THE NOSE
This is a widespread
action in which the
nostrils are pinched
between the thumb
and first finger of
one hand (**2**), as if
trying to shut out a
horrible smell.
People do this to
show that some
object or idea is so
bad it metaphorically
stinks.

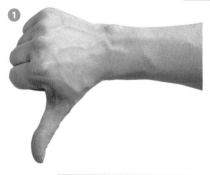

Pulling a chain A British version involves pulling an imaginary chain down with one hand as if flushing an old-fashioned lavatory, while pinching the nostrils with the other (**3**).

WRINKLING THE NOSE
The nose is wrinkled as if trying to shut out a nasty smell (the disgusted facial expression, see p. 32). This is another widespread way of displaying a low or negative opinion of something or someone.

SHRUGGING

Shrugging is how we sign 'I don't know', 'I don't understand', 'I can't help' or 'It's none of my business'. The full shrug mimics the hunched attitude assumed by someone who feels under threat, though he or she offers no opposition. But shrugging takes several forms: some of these are described below.

1 Hunching the shoulders This widespread jerky action is made while raising the eyebrows, pulling down both corners of the mouth, and holding the hands out palm upwards. The head might be tilted to one side.

2 Turning down the corners of the mouth
This abbreviated shrug is common in France.

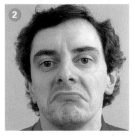

3 Holding out both the hands Here the palms face upwards, with fingers slightly curled. This is widespread. The facial expression exhibited is similar to that shown in **1** and **2**.

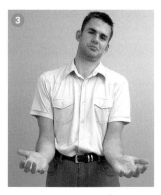

4 Raising an open hand The hand is raised, palm outwards, to shoulder height, while both shoulders shrug slightly. The facial expression is similar to those shown above.

LACK OF INTEREST

CONTRACTION OF THE EYES' PUPILS
This is a subconscious signal. A person whose pupils shrink probably is not interested in the situation or person he or she is currently involved with.

INDIFFERENCE
Indifference can be betrayed by a seemingly relaxed attitude. For example, a man (it is usually a man) who is indifferent to a person or situation might sit very casually, with one leg flung over the arm of his chair (**1**; he could also be signalling dominance or hostility, see p. 170.)

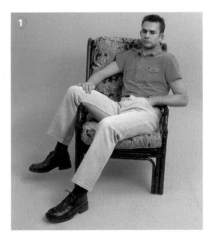

INATTENTION

The following examples occur when two people are talking to each other but one is not paying attention to what the other is saying.

Scanning away The individual who is not paying attention probably spends less time looking at the other person than in other directions (**2**).

Head turning The individual who is not paying attention might keep turning the head away from the other person.

Asymmetrical smiling The individual not paying attention might respond to the other's remarks with lopsided smiles (**3**).

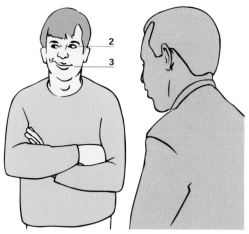

REJECTION

If someone is buttonholed at a meeting or party by another person they would rather avoid, the first person is likely to give stronger hints of rejection than by merely showing lack of attention, or by assuming one of the defensive postures described in Chapter 9. The second person will probably realize they are being rejected by the first, if he or she

- half turns the body and head away;
- assumes a blank expression;
- stares pointedly into the middle distance so that the other person cannot catch his or her eye to try to keep the talk flowing;
- puts a hand up to the mouth to stifle a pretended (or genuine) yawn;
- openly yawns, pouts or sneers;
- fidgets, picks fingernails or teeth, or makes finger joints crack;
- openly disagrees with the bore by shaking the head; and, ultimately,
- turns away and walks off.

BOREDOM

When seated people are bored by a dry talk or a dull television programme, they assume tell-tale postures that give away what they are feeling.

- The head turns to one side now and then.
- The head begins to need some support from a hand.
- The trunk becomes straighter.
- The legs become straighter.

LOSING INTEREST
The following sequence illustrates how declining interest might be betrayed.

- The head is completely propped up by a hand.
- The person leans back.
- The legs are fully stretched.
- A bored individual trying not to look bored might lean forward.
- If boredom is extreme, the person might close their eyes and assume a very slumped posture.

SIGNS OF BOREDOM
Besides the actions and postures just mentioned, people signal boredom in ways such as those listed below and on the following pages.

1 Twiddling the thumbs A widespread, subconscious gesture of boredom, the fingers are interlocked and the thumbs circle each other.

2 Measuring an imaginary beard

This is done with the hand and implies that the speaker has droned on long enough for the listener to grow a beard. Bored men sometimes do this in Italy, Germany and the Netherlands.

3 Rubbing the cheek

The backs of the fingers are rubbed to and fro against the cheek, as if feeling stubble. This is largely a French gesture.

4 Tapping the chest slowly with one hand The hand is held sideways, pointing down, with the thumb facing the body. Bored Italians sometimes do this to indicate that someone's talking is giving them indigestion.

FEELING FED UP

Several gestures signal 'I've had it up to here'.

1 Tapping under the chin This is done with the back of the hand and is a way of showing that a person has suffered more than he or she can stand. This is an American and West European gesture.

2 Sawing the hand to and fro across the throat Made with the side of a hand, this is an Austrian equivalent of tapping oneself under the chin.

3 Tapping the top of the head repeatedly Done with the palm of the hand, this is the strongest South American way of expressing 'I am fed up'.

IMPATIENCE

Feelings of impatience are often given away by fidgety movements involving fingers, thighs or feet. As substitutes for walking or running, these actions might occur with some of the 'getting ready' actions described in the next chapter. They are seen almost worldwide.

DRUMMING THE FINGERS
An individual who is sitting with a hand resting on a table or arm of a chair might signal impatience by drumming his or her fingers in rapid succession (**1**).

FOOT FIDGETING
A standing person might repeatedly tap his or her foot on the ground. Alternatively, if sitting with legs crossed, the individual may twitch the suspended foot up and down (**2**).

SLAPPING A THIGH
A person standing might repeatedly slap an open hand against the outside of one thigh (**3**).

SARCASM

Sarcastic gestures are mocking ways of showing approval or enthusiasm.

DISTORTED SMILING
One corner of the mouth is pulled in so strongly that the cheek is puckered (**1**). This lopsided smile could betray that a person is pretending to show friendly approval when he or she is really feeling hostile and contemptuous. In the Western world, people can express sarcasm like this. This kind of smile can also signal inattention (see p. 120).

CLAPPING WITH THUMBNAILS

The thumbnails are repeatedly patted together (**2**) as if clapping the hands in miniature. In Latin America, Spain and the Netherlands, thumbnail clapping is a form of ironic applause, which tends to be used when the real thing would normally be expected.

THE PURSED HAND

Lowering a pursed hand (**3**) once is a sarcastic Maltese way of saying 'good', when an individual really means 'You idiot!'

DISBELIEF

People in several parts of the world have special ways of showing they do not believe what someone is telling them.

STROKING THE THROAT
A South American gesture of disbelief involves stroking the front of the neck up and down repeatedly with a first finger (**1**). The action implies that the remarks coming from an associate's throat are rubbish.

POINTING AT A HAND
The first finger of one hand is pointed at the other, which is held open, palm upwards (**2**). This Jewish gesture means 'My hand will sprout grass before what you say comes to pass'.

RAISING A
TROUSER LEG
Holding one trouser
leg above the thigh,
a man delicately lifts
it as if he has just
stepped in a heap of
dung (**3**). American
men might do this
as a playful way of
saying that what
they have just been
told is a load of
manure.

SHARING NEGATIVE INFORMATION

Friends or acquaintances often use gestures when they
want to share negative information or an opinion about
another individual, without letting them or others know
what they are saying. Several examples of types of gesture
from around the world used to hint at complicity,
suspicion or contempt of another, and to make derogatory
sexual comments, are illustrated below. Certain signs,
however, have more than one meaning which depends
upon where they are used.

HINTS OF COMPLICITY

- Winking one eye is how many Europeans and North Americans show they are sharing a secret (or a light-hearted deception; **1**).
- Tapping one side of the nose with an index finger (**2**) can mean 'Keep this quiet – just between the two of us'. It is common in Britain and Italy. This, like winking, does not necessarily mean that the secret shared is negative.

Tapping the nose: alternative meanings Tapping the nose can be used to

- warn another person that someone is nosey in Italy, France, Spain and the Netherlands;
- mean 'Mind your own business' in the British Isles, Austria and Belgium;
- mean 'I'm on to you!' or 'I know what's going on' in northern Belgium and, rarely, in other parts of Europe; and
- praise someone else's alertness or shrewdness in Sicily and Southern Italy.

SIGNS OF SUSPICION

- Pulling the lower eyelid down to make the eye appear bigger (**3**) is how an Italian or Spaniard might say 'Watch out: be on your guard'. This gesture does, however, have a positive meaning in South America (see p. 105).

- Patting the elbow with the hand of the other arm (**4**) is Dutch for 'Don't rely on him'. Compare this with the Dutch 'Get lost!' gesture on p. 140. There is a subtle difference between them.

DISPARAGING COMMENTS

- Rolling the eyes to show the whites and raising the eyebrows (**5**) means 'Would you believe it?'; or, when a forgetful person starts repeating an often-told anecdote, 'There she goes again'.

- Tapping the temple or forehead (**6**; the exact spot can vary from country to country) can mean 'He's crazy'.

8. Signs of conflict

If disagreement and disapproval lead on to personal dislike and enmity, signs of conflict can evolve from unconsciously critical postures and actions through deliberate insults to openly threatening behaviour that may lead to violence.

HIDDEN DISAPPROVAL OR DISAGREEMENT

Someone who objects to the views another person is expressing might not feel free to say so. Instead, he or she might betray the negative feelings with silent and apparently insignificant actions that seem to have no connection with the matter in hand.

POSTURES

Lowering the head
A critical listener is likely to tilt the forehead forward (**1**). Lowering the head like this seems a chance action, but implies that the listener dislikes or disagrees with what the speaker is saying.

Closed posture
A seated individual who disagrees with the speaker is likely to adopt a so-called closed posture by folding the arms, crossing one leg over the other above the knee, and holding the head and body straight (**2**).

GESTURES

Rubbing an eye Someone might frequently rub an eye or pull at an eyelid while sitting in a bored attitude (see pp. 121–2). Arguably, feedback from such critical postures to their owner's brain reinforces and prolongs a critical frame of mind.

Lint picking
The disapproving listener might pick at his or her clothing with finger and thumb as if to remove an invisible bit of fluff or piece of thread (**3**). Instead of looking at the speaker, the lint picker may stare at the floor. These little actions reveal that he or she is nursing unspoken objections.

OPEN DISAPPROVAL OR DISAGREEMENT

Someone who dislikes another person's ideas or attitudes and feels no need to hide this feeling may show it in unmistakable actions, three of which are described below.

EYE BEHAVIOUR AND GESTURES

Glancing sideways Someone who glances sideways at another person, with a downturned mouth, creased brow and lowered eyebrows, may well be thinking something critical about the individual, what he or she stands for, or what he or she is saying.

Turning the nose
Someone who disbelieves or dislikes what another is saying might show it by twitching muscles that momentarily pull the nose slightly sideways (**1**), as if moving it away from a disagreeable smell.

Pointing both first fingers Pointing the tip of each extended first finger at the other, and moving them towards and away from each other (**2**) is a Spanish or Latin American way of signalling disagreement.

INSULTS

Body language includes a huge repertoire of insulting gestures, mainly involving head and hand. The examples given here include several with a strong regional flavour.

INSULTS MADE WITH
THE HEAD
Head tapping A person repeatedly taps his or her head with a first finger (**1**). More than one finger may be used. Though the person tapping the forehead or temple points to his or her own brain, the suggestion is that there is something wrong with someone else's.

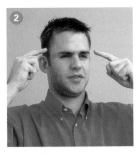

Two-handed head tapping Both sides of the forehead are tapped by both hands (**2**). This expresses strong irritation with another person's stupidity.

Circling a first finger by a temple The person points at the temple and makes small circling movements (**3**), suggesting a disorganized or scrambled brain, or one run down like a clock that needs winding up.

Poking out the tongue One person simply faces another he or she wants to insult and pokes the tongue out towards them (**4**). Like shaking the head for 'no', this stems from an infant's food-rejection actions. It is widespread among children but seen among some groups of adults as well.

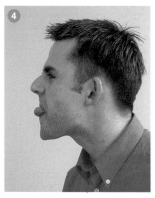

INSULTS MADE WITH THE ARMS

Striking the elbow The right hand is held up, the outside edge facing forward. The back of the left hand is tapped against the right elbow and at the same time the right hand is brought down in a quick chopping motion (**5**). This Dutch gesture means 'Get lost!'

Striking the wrist As the left hand performs a chopping motion on the right wrist, the right hand is flicked upwards (**6**). Another 'Go away!' signal, this is used mainly in Mediterranean nations such as Tunisia and Greece. It is probably based on the punitive action of chopping off a thief's hand before expelling him or her from the community.

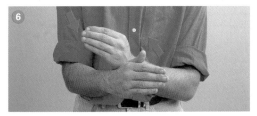

INSULTS MADE WITH THE HANDS

The hand push An open hand, fingers stretched out and apart, is pushed at the face of the person being insulted (**7**). Known as the moutza, this is an old Greek 'Go to hell!' insult. It is derived from the Byzantine practice of humiliating convicts or prisoners of war by scooping up handfuls of muck from the street and shoving it into their faces.

The V sign The V sign (**8**) is a mainly British gesture. It means 'Up yours!' Most people intend this as a sexual insult, but it reputedly began as a defiant gesture made by medieval English archers after their French enemies had threatened to amputate their bowstring fingers.

SIGNS OF HOSTILITY

Sometimes, dislike grows strong enough to lead to open conflict. There are warning signs of possible fighting ahead, mainly male examples of which are given below.

SUMMING EACH OTHER UP

Two men who are strangers and feeling unsure of themselves might try to proclaim their masculinity by standing with hands on hips, or fingers or thumbs tucked into the front of the belt, a gesture which draws attention to the genital region. Some researchers claim this posture means 'I can dominate you because I am virile'. If the men are merely sizing each other up in friendly conversation, they might stand half facing each other (1).

GETTING READY TO FIGHT

If they stand face to face, however, with their feet apart, and have placed hands on hips or tucked fingers or thumbs into a belt or pocket top, they might dislike one another and they could be spoiling for a fight.

STOPPING SHORT OF A FIGHT

Two enemies might make aggressive gestures rather than hit each other. These threats may be directed by one person at another, or at someone or something else.

1 Fist shaking The individual punches the air in front of the enemy.

2 Arm raising The person raises an arm as if about to hit the enemy, but stops short.

Other actions include a person hitting his or her own hand or banging a fist down onto a table.

9. Domination and defensiveness

This chapter looks at how people sometimes try to dominate and intimidate one another. It also describes some of the unconscious defensive postures people adopt when they are feeling under attack, emotionally uncomfortable or hostile. Some conscious defensive actions – gestures made to prevent ill-luck – are examined too.

DOMINATING OTHERS

A person with an intention to dominate someone else might unconsciously use or emphasize certain gestures when greeting or escorting that person. This kind of domination is often benign. Invasion of personal space (see p. 60) is a more blatant and hostile form of domination, which may be deliberately used to intimidate.

THE DOMINANT HANDSHAKE
When one person extends a hand for a handshake, with palm facing downwards, this generally forces the other individual to shake with the palm of the hand in an upturned, submissive position (**1**). This is a dominant handshake. Businesspeople might use it when they want to control an interaction.

THE FIRM HANDSHAKE
In a handshake between two dominant individuals, each might literally try to gain the upper hand. The result is a firm grip with vertical palms and parallel thumbs (**2**). If

each person is aggressively dominant, the grip could be vice-like. Generally in the West, the firm handshake is seen as a sign of sincerity (see p. 82)

GUIDING

A host ushering a guest into a room full of people wants to guide the guest towards a particular person or group. To do this the host might, for instance, place the palm of an open hand on the guest's back between the shoulder blades and press lightly, steering the guest in the right direction (**3**). In this interaction, host and guest's roles echo those of parent and child (see p. 63).

SEAT STRADDLING
A forceful individual who wants to butt in on a group conversation and try to control it might use, curiously, a defensive method. This method involves sitting astride a chair so that the person's arms rest on its back (**4**). While feeling physically protected by the chair back from other group members' potential hostility, the straddler may feel better able to take a dominant, if not domineering, attitude in the group conversation.

UNCONSCIOUS DEFENSIVE ACTIONS

Certain situations prove particularly uncomfortable. For instance, many people feel uneasy trying to disagree with domineering individuals at a business conference, meeting the firm's chairman at a Christmas party, greeting a large crowd of unfamiliar guests or making a wedding speech. As children, dangers like these might have driven us to hide behind our mother or a large piece of furniture. As adults, we might unconsciously put up protective portable barriers, usually using our own arms or legs. Some researchers claim these barriers are really a form of reassuring self-clasping, a protective action rooted in the comfort derived by a baby from its mother's embrace.

DEFENSIVE HAND AND ARM GESTURES

Crossing the arms in front of the body is an almost instinctive attempt to protect the heart and lungs against threat. Researchers have identified several main protective arm-crossing postures.

1 Basic crossed arms Both arms are folded across the chest with one forearm crossing the other, so that one hand rests on an upper arm and the other hand is tucked between elbow and chest. We tend to do this whenever we feel slightly anxious, for instance, standing in a crowded lift or a queue.

2 Gripped crossed arms Both arms are folded across the chest and each hand is clasped tightly around an upper arm. Nervous air travellers waiting for take-off and anxious patients waiting to see a doctor might grip their arms in this way.

3 Crossed arms with clenched fists The arms are crossed and the fists clenched. The teeth might also be clenched. People who do this could be so angry that their defensive hostility is on the point of giving way to aggression.

4 Incomplete crossed arms One arm crosses the body and the hand clasps the other arm (which is hanging down) or the back of the other hand. A person who does this may be recreating a childhood feeling of safety when a parent held his or her hand. People tend to hold hands with themselves when facing an audience.

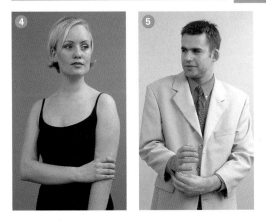

5 Masked crossed arms The arms are moved protectively across the body but the gesture is made to appear incidental to some other action. Here are three examples.

- Moving a hand across the body to check the clasp of a handbag in the other hand.

- Using both hands to hold a wine glass.

- Using one hand to make a pretended adjustment to a shirtsleeve button or cufflink.

Gestures like these are often performed, for example, by media personalities, politicians and members of the British royal family when they are trying to conceal feelings of uncertainty.

DEFENSIVE LEG GESTURES
Crossing the legs or ankles can also signal that a person tends to feel on the defensive. This time the genital area is the zone being defended. People feeling defensive (or negative) often cross their legs to reinforce a crossed-arms barrier. Merely crossing the legs, though, suggests less strongly defensive (or negative) feelings than just crossing the arms. Like arm-crossing, crossing the legs or ankles can take several forms.

1 Crossed knees, standing One leg is crossed in front of the other. This stance can often be seen at gatherings where people might not know each other too well, and so are mildly anxious.

2 Crossed knees, sitting The back of one knee is hooked over the front of the other. If a boyfriend annoys his girlfriend, for example, she might stay sitting beside him but shift to the defensive/ negative crossed-knees and folded-arms posture. Beware misinterpreting: many people in an audience sit like this to listen to a talk or a musical performance.

3 Shin cross, sitting (overleaf) Researchers identify this as a mainly male posture, although women do use it. The ankle end of the shin of one leg rests across the knee of the other leg and is at right angles to it. In fact, this posture can be more combative than defensive. A member of an audience, who is at first sitting defensively while listening to an aggressive speaker, might suddenly assume the shin-cross posture when he wants to dispute a point. This is likelier among, say, British or Australian men than American men, who commonly sit in this way. In some parts of the world, this sitting position is insulting.

4 Clamped shin cross, sitting Both hands clasp the shin crossed over the other leg's knee. People tend to sit like this during a discussion when they are strongly defending their views and unwilling to change them.

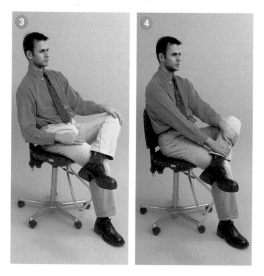

5 Ankle cross One ankle is crossed over the other. Men and women tend to cross their ankles when they are nervous or negative but trying to suppress these feelings.

6 Foot lock, standing Researchers identify this as a mainly female posture. One leg is drawn up so that its foot presses against the calf of the supporting leg. A person might assume this posture when resisting a sales proposition.

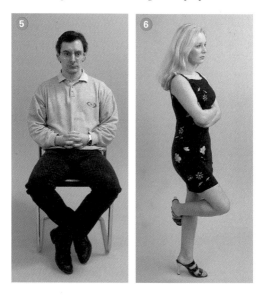

7 Foot lock, sitting
One foot is drawn up behind the other leg and pressed against its calf. This is the seated equivalent of the standing foot lock.

CONSCIOUS DEFENSIVE ACTIONS

Good-luck gestures are the most familiar conscious defensive actions.

GOOD-LUCK GESTURES
Most people worry about the outcome of certain events such as securing a rise in pay, winning promotion or having a baby. Superstitious people, and many who claim they are not, perform special actions to bring good luck or protection against bad luck or hostile supernatural influence.

Crossing the fingers The second finger is crossed over the first finger of the same hand, and the thumb pressed against the other fingers, which are tucked into the palm (**1**). This 'good luck' sign originated as a symbol of the cross on which Christ died, and was made by Christians asking for God's protection. It is widespread, but especially common in Britain and Scandinavia.

Making two fists Both hands are lowered and made into fists with the thumbs tucked inside (**2**). This is a German 'good luck' gesture equivalent to crossing the fingers.

10. Tension and relaxation

This chapter is about the body language that betrays nervousness and depression – feelings often prompted by some kind of emotional stress. (See also Chapter 11 for the signals that help to betray people who are stressed because they are lying.) Here, signs of relaxation and feeling at ease are also examined.

SIGNS OF EMOTIONAL DISCOMFORT

FEELING SO-SO
People in the United States and Europe who are feeling less than happy might respond to someone else's 'How are you?' by holding out an open hand, palm down, fingers spread out, and rocking it (**1**). This gesture often accompanies a phrase such as 'Oh, so-so.'

FEELING FED UP

When asked how he or she is, an overworked person might say, 'I've had it up to here,' and demonstrate where 'here' is by raising an open hand, palm down, to their forehead (**2**). The hand indicates the level of the imaginary water in which they are drowning.

FEELING SELF-CRITICAL OR EMBARRASSED

When people realise they have done something silly, they might say they have been so stupid they could hit themselves. The phrase might be accompanied by a mock blow with an open hand to their own head, which usually falls on one of four places:

- the side of the face (**3**);
- the forehead (**4**);
- the top of the head (**5**); or
- the back of the neck (**6**).

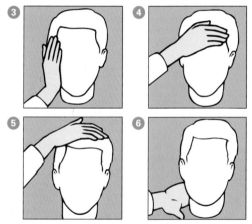

Research suggests that where the blow falls shows more than merely self-criticism. If an employee reprimanded for carelessness hits the forehead, the boss's criticism is probably not a serious worry. If the employee slaps the back of the neck, he or she might really think the boss is a 'pain in the neck' for exposing the error.

Poking out the tongue
In southern China and Tibet, someone who has spoken out of turn might acknowledge a feeling of embarrassment by poking the tongue tip out fleetingly (**7**).

FEELING SUICIDAL
If they make a social gaffe or everything seems to be going wrong in their lives, people sometimes say they feel almost suicidal. As they speak they make the gesture of killing themselves (often in a joking context). The gesture used varies with the method of suicide favoured in a particular region.

Worldwide A worldwide gesture to reflect suicidal feelings involves dragging a first finger across the throat as if wounding it with an old-fashioned cutthroat razor (**8**). This gesture is also used widely as a threat.

In the West A
Western action
involves pointing a
first finger to the
side of the head
with the thumb
up, like the
hammer of a
revolver, and then
bringing the
thumb down (**9**).

In New Guinea
A New Guinea
islander might
grasp the throat,
mimicking a
strangling
action (**10**).

In Japan A Japanese man may 'chop' himself in the belly with the side of a flat hand held palm upwards (**11**). This action mimicks hara-kiri: the traditional male Japanese method of ritual suicide by disembowelment with a sword.

FEELING DEPRESSED
People feeling dejected (**12**) might:

- take short, dragging steps;
- keep both hands in their pockets; and/or
- keep the head bowed.

Contented people can also walk like this if their minds are busy solving problems.

DISPLACEMENT ACTIVITIES

When people feel uncertain, tense or nervous (or bored, see pp. 121–4 and 135), they unconsciously tend to perform trivial and useless actions. These have been categorized by Desmond Morris as 'displacement activities'. Many occur in everyday situations. Some include a reassuring self-touching component.

TYPICAL DISPLACEMENT ACTIVITIES
These cover a wide range of actions where the nervous person's hands, feet or eyes make fiddly, purposeless movements. Here are examples of the actions that might be seen in a doctor's or dentist's waiting room, among candidates waiting to be interviewed for a job or in a traffic jam. All of them are believed by researchers to indicate tension in terms of frustration and nervousness.

- Putting a hand up to a tie as if adjusting it, even though the tie is quite straight.
- Tapping a chair arm with a finger, or the floor with a foot.
- Twisting a ring around on a finger (**1**), and perhaps removing and replacing it.

- Scratching the head.
- Pinching an eyelid (**2**).
- Sitting slumped, staring at the floor or a spot on the wall opposite.

Oral displacement activities Researchers suggest that these are unconscious attempts to recapture the sense of security that people felt as babies when being nursed at their mothers' breasts. Three examples are given below.

- Biting a fingernail (**3**) or chewing a thumb.
- Sucking a pen or pencil while making notes.
- Removing spectacles and putting one end in the mouth (**4**).

SMOKERS' DISPLACEMENT ACTIVITIES

Many smokers who lead stressful lives say that smoking calms them down. This may be only partly because it provides a nicotine 'fix'. The act of smoking can also give the smoker the opportunity to perform reassuring displacement activities, such as those described below.

- Sucking on a cigarette, cigar or pipe is the smoker's equivalent of the non-smoker's thumb chewing or pen sucking.

- The nervous cigarette smoker might keep tapping a cigarette on an ashtray to knock off the ash.

- The pipe smoker might make a prolonged ritual out of cleaning, filling and lighting a pipe.

SHUTTING OUT THE WORLD

Sometimes we suffer greater stress than can be relieved by crossing our arms or legs (see p. 147) or performing little displacement activities. At such times, people might resort to one of the following ways of shutting out whatever is worrying them.

EYE 'CUT-OFFS'

Someone under great stress might display any of four types of unconscious eye behaviour.

Eye avoidance Although talking and listening to another person, the tense individual fixes the gaze somewhere else for much of the time (**1**).

Eye shifting The stressed person's gaze is rapidly and continuously switched to and from another who is speaking.

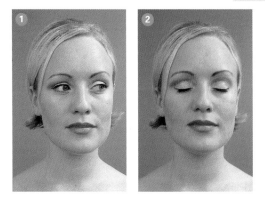

Eyelid fluttering The listener looks the speaker in the eye, but now and then the listener's eyelids go into spasms of fluttering up and down.

Eyelid closing The anxious listener looks the speaker in the eye but now and then a momentary blink is extended by several seconds (**2**).

Shutting-out eye behaviour sometimes indicates something more specific than general stress (see p. 121).

COCOONING
Stressed individuals sometimes try to retreat into worlds of their own. Two examples of cocooning are given below.

Mild cocooning For example, an individual studying in a library might try to block out distracting sights by resting

the elbows on a table, and propping up the head on the thumbs and first fingers of both hands, forming blinkers for the eyes (**3**).

Extreme cocooning
This form of self-hugging, in which the person is curled up tightly, the head buried in the drawn-up, tightly embraced knees (**4**), is thought by researchers to be an attempt to shut out external horrors completely. People overwhelmed by a disaster, such as the death of a close relative or the loss of everything they own, might be seen doing this.

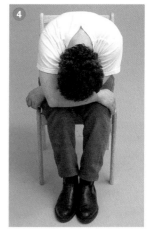

FEELING AT EASE

People who are comfortable with the situation they find themselves in behave quite differently from those under stress. If they are fully awake, their gestures and actions are likely to be more expansive and less defensive than those of someone who is nervous or tense. When they relax they are more likely to slump and 'let themselves go' than an individual who feels ill at ease and constrained.

BECOMING RELAXED

Students of human behaviour have observed that people change their postures and gestures as they become more relaxed in social situations.

THE THAWING-OUT PROCESS

Usually, as they get to know one another, strangers lose their initial shyness. In much of the Western world, this thawing-out process might be seen to pass through stages such as those detailed below.

- The strangers may stand well apart from each other at first, with crossed legs and arms (**1**, overleaf). If they are wearing them, the buttons of their jackets or coats might be done up, even if it is not at all cold.

- After a while, the strangers might uncross their legs and stand with their feet pointing slightly outward. Their arms will probably still be crossed.

- Each talker might begin to gesticulate with the hand of the uppermost arm. After gesticulating, instead of folding the hand back under the other arm, the speaker might leave it resting on top.

- As tension diminishes, each speaker might uncross the arms, thrusting one hand into a pocket or gesticulating with it to stress the points being made (**2**).

- Later still comes unbuttoning of jackets or coats. Each individual might push a foot forward towards the person

he or she feels most concerned with, while the back foot bears most of the body's weight.

- As the strangers become acquaintances, they may move closer together until they are well within each other's personal zones (see p. 49).

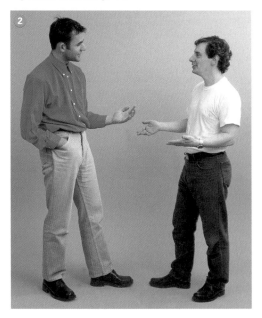

SIGNS OF RELAXATION

The way in which people relax (if they relax) in company gives clues to their attitudes and relationships with the people around them.

AMONG ACQUAINTANCES

If a person assumes a very relaxed body posture, sprawling on a sofa, for example, while conversing with people he or she doesn't know very well, this will probably be taken by the others as lack of courtesy or an extreme show of dominance. Both are generally found threatening. Largely to avoid this jarring kind of interaction, most of us only partly relax in the majority of social situations. We choose to *seem* alert, and 'switched-on' and receptive to those around us. For example, a person at a gathering might sit quite upright with shins or legs crossed but with the hands clasped lightly resting in the lap (**1**). If so, then he or she is displaying body language of reasonable openness.

AMONG CLOSE FRIENDS

When among close friends or relatives, individuals usually feel free to relax completely. The signs of being at ease are generally reflected by open body language, which might include slumped postures, seen when people lie on the floor or sprawl on a sofa (**2**).

11. Sincerity and deceit

How do you know when people are telling the truth and when they are lying? How can you tell when they are saying what they really feel, and are not just being polite? The answer could be by checking their words against their body language to make sure both agree. For the body has its own silent ways of saying 'I am telling the truth', 'I am hiding something', 'I am telling lies' – and these are often more reliable guides than speech.

SHOWING SINCERITY

IN GENERAL INTERACTION

When we want to convince someone that what we are saying is true, we tend to look them in the eye and gesticulate with our hands, holding them out palms upwards, showing we have nothing to hide. People usually perform this action unconsciously to reinforce a remark such as 'Believe me' or 'Honestly, nothing else happened'.

FORMALIZED SIGNALS OF SINCERITY

The open hand as a sign of trustworthiness is old and widespread, as the examples below remind us.

Hailing and waving People wave open palms at each other as they approach (see p. 78). The original purpose of this action was to show that the individuals were unarmed.

Handshaking People meeting shake hands palm-to-palm (see pp. 79–80). The original purpose was again to show the lack of weapons. Individuals sometimes choose to amplify their handshakes to underline the sincerity of their greeting.

Oath taking Muslims and Christians swearing an oath tend to raise the right hand shoulder high with the hand open and palm facing forward (**1**).

Swearing loyalty A United States citizen swearing loyalty to the Stars and Stripes places the right hand on the heart (**2**), to show that it belongs to the nation. This 'hand on heart' gesture dates back to ancient Greece where slaves used it to show loyalty to their owners.

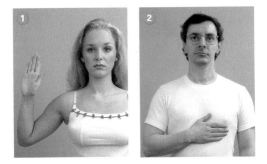

DECEIVING OTHERS

People often deceive each other on many social occasions and in everyday encounters. For instance, a guest who loathes the food at a party might pretend to enjoy it to avoid offending the host.

DETECTING DECEPTION

Effective lying involves not only speaking as naturally as possible but matching the body language with the spoken words. It is difficult to suppress the tell-tale movements that the body and limbs make unconsciously, and the genuinely felt expressions that fleetingly appear on the face. Researchers claim that the body's unspoken signals carry five times more weight than the spoken word, so when speech and body language are at odds, deceit is a possible reason. It's not the only one, though: an action may reveal that someone feels tense rather than deceitful.

SIGNS OF DECEIT

Tests performed with a group of subjects helped to show which actions and postures give us the most and least reliable clues to deception. Here is a list beginning with the least reliable indicators and ending with the most trustworthy ones.

- Facial expressions
- Deliberate actions
- Gesticulations
- Self-touching
- Leg and foot actions
- Gaze behaviour
- Autonomic nervous system reactions such as blushing

All but the last sign are explained fully below and on the following pages.

FACIAL EXPRESSIONS

These are the easiest to control, and therefore the hardest to read. Skilled liars can look convincingly happy or sad. In one test, people watching the subjects' facial expressions wrongly guessed who was lying more often than not. But years of research into facial expression led psychologist Paul Ekman to discover the following clues to revealing a hidden emotion or one that is faked.

Fleeting expressions These are genuinely felt expressions that flit across someone's face in less than one-fifth of a second. Such a micro-expression might momentarily replace a smile with a look of sadness or anger. Most of us register micro-expressions only unconsciously. This helps to explain why sometimes we have an uneasy feeling that a person dislikes us even while apparently being friendly.

Suppressed expressions These are genuinely felt expressions that begin to form until people realize what is happening and replace them with the expressions they prefer others to see. Suppressed expressions appear more often than micro-expressions and last longer so they are easier to spot, but skilled liars are usually careful not to let their true feelings sneak out in this way.

Dependable facial muscles These are the facial muscles least under their owner's control, and so the most dependable for showing the observer what their owner is feeling. People can try to mask their effects, for instance by smiling, but dependable muscles – especially those in the forehead – are likely to let true feelings show. The three examples below illustrate how the dependable muscles can betray someone's true feelings, though they might be smiling.

- The eyebrows' inner corners might rise, and wrinkles appear in the middle of the forehead, betraying sadness (**1**).
- The eyebrows might rise and come together, betraying fear or worry (**2**).
- The lips might narrow and the eyebrows be pulled downwards and inwards, betraying anger (**3**).

Even 'dependable' muscles are not always reliable. Skilled habitual liars can suppress them, and innocent people suspected of lying may show a fear reaction similar to that seen in a genuine liar.

Phoney smiles

People can fake a smile to express an emotion such as amusement, contentment, enjoyment, pleasure or relief when they are feeling none of these things. Family photographs often show us only too clearly smiles that look false, yet we usually find it hard to analyse why.
Manwatching

author Desmond Morris suggests a false smile differs from a felt smile because it tends to 'fall short' in several ways.

A REAL SMILE (1)

- is of a certain strength
- grows to full strength at a certain rate and fades at a certain rate according to strength
- lasts for a correct length of time according to its strength
- is symmetrical, with lips stretched and both corners of the mouth raised
- affects the rest of the face to the right degree: it creates crow's feet wrinkles at the eyes' corners; forms bags under the eyes; and lowers the eyebrows

A FALSE SMILE MAY

- be of an incorrect strength
- appear far too quickly or far too slowly
- fail to last for the correct amount of time: it may either be far too short (the on-off smile) or far too long (the frozen smile)
- be asymmetrical or crooked, with only one corner of the mouth raised (2)
- not affect other parts of the face, such as the eyes or cheeks, to the degree seen in a real smile (3)

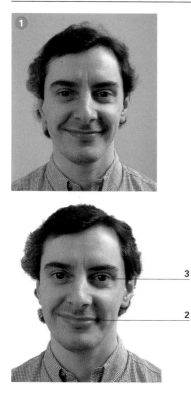

DELIBERATE ACTIONS

Head, hand or shoulder actions that represent words (for
example, nodding the head for 'yes', and the thumb and
finger ring sign for 'OK') are unreliable guides to
someone's emotion or attitude because people can make
such gestures deliberately. Yet people sometimes let slip a
gesture which says something they would rather keep
hidden.

**The incomplete
gesture** Guests
asked if they
would like to see
their host's holiday
video film, for
example, might
say 'yes' but betray
their reluctance
with an
incomplete shrug.
This might involve
slightly lifting one
shoulder or briefly
exposing the
palms of the hands
to signify 'I'm
powerless to say
no' (**1**).

**The disguised
gesture** Instead of
shrugging by

extending the arms and spreading the hands, an individual might just turn the hands palms upwards in his or her lap. Instead of thrusting a middle finger vertically upwards to say 'Up yours!', a frustrated person might unconsciously make this gesture with a finger resting on a knee (**2**).

GESTICULATIONS

People concealing the truth or their innermost feelings are sometimes betrayed by their gesticulations. Their hands might unconsciously reflect their feelings as they speak.

For instance, a nervous politician's supplicatory palms-up hand display would contradict his claim to be determined and confident. Liars therefore tend to stifle uncontrolled give-away hand movements by holding both hands together or thrusting them in their pockets. In particular, they tend to conceal the palms of the hands. A child denying it has eaten a jar of sweets might hide its hands behind its back; an unfaithful spouse might stand with arms folded, protesting his or her innocence. Gesticulation is natural, so the keen observer might well be suspicious when it is lacking or muted. But we must also remember that skilful liars can give a convincing performance of the 'honest' palms-up display.

SELF-TOUCHING
The deceitful person who gesticulates less than normal might, nonetheless, make small, self-touching movements. Most involve putting a hand to the head – especially the mouth, or an eye or ear – or neck, as if the liar were trying not to speak, see or hear an untruth. The deception might involve a serious lie or just concealed panic as someone mentally grapples with a difficult question. Of course, the actions described here and on the following pages may be the result of habit, nervousness, fright or a physical need, such as the need to scratch an itch.

Concealing the mouth Young children who catch themselves lying tend to cover the mouth with both hands (**1**). Adults who find themselves doing this tend to use a weakened form of mouth concealment: they touch the cheek, nose (**2**) or forehead instead. They might appear to be rubbing an itchy spot, but their scratching is weak and unfocused.

Rubbing an eye
Closing both eyes and rubbing the eyelid of one is how a liar might react to avoid eye contact with the companion being deceived. Allan Pease remarks that men tend to rub an eye vigorously (**3**), looking at the floor if telling a 'whopper', while women gently massage the skin under the eye, and look at the ceiling.

Rubbing an ear There are several variants: pulling an ear lobe (**4**), caressing the back of the ear and rotating a fingertip stuck in the ear. According to Allan Pease, these are all adult equivalents of a child's covering both ears to avoid being scolded for telling a lie.

Rubbing the neck

Rubbing or scratching the back of the neck (**5**) or pulling the collar (**6**) are additional self-touching actions performed by people who may not be telling the truth or who might be keeping something back. For example, neck rubbing might be performed by someone who really disagrees with another though he or she is voicing agreement.

LEG AND FOOT ACTIONS
Desmond Morris considers leg and foot movements
among the more reliable signs of deceit. This is largely
because we tend to focus on faces and hands, and forget
that the lower limbs can also betray secret feelings. Like a
restless body, fidgety leg and foot movements can show a
wish to be gone (see pp. 126–7). For example, a woman
who rubs one leg with the other – believed by some
researchers to be an erotic form of self-touching – might
be hinting that she feels less demure than her facial
expression would have the observer believe.

GAZE BEHAVIOUR
Direction of gaze may reveal hidden emotion or
information withheld. Companions whose eyes meet our
gaze for less than one-third of the time might be
concealing information from us. (If they are Japanese or
Korean, though, they are probably being polite.) Skilled
liars can make frequent eye contact.

BODY SHIFTS

Liars or people withholding information tend to fidget in
their chairs, perhaps leaning first one way then another, as
if they want to get away from the situation. Bored people
pretending interest are likely to give themselves away by
their slumped posture (see p. 121).

12. Animal gestures

Many animals use body language of some kind – even if only to turn to face each other when they meet, sizing one another up in readiness for a friendly or unfriendly encounter. Most creatures can convey only a few basic signals by posture or gesture, but human bodies are uniquely equipped for sending many more silent messages.

EVOLUTION AND BODY LANGUAGE

Our complex body language is a result of the gradual changes that led from fish, through amphibians and reptiles, to mammals, which of course include humans.

THE PRIMATE INHERITANCE

It is largely from prehistoric apes, close kin to living chimpanzees, that we humans derive our tendency to express our feelings by posture and gesticulation. Chimpanzees, like humans, are social animals that live in groups. To cooperate for survival and to keep the wheels of their societies turning smoothly, they need to communicate. They use mainly nonvocal means – posture, facial expression and touching gestures – to signal dominance or submission, friendliness or hostility. Some actions performed by chimpanzees are almost identical to ours in similar circumstances. Two examples are given below.

- One chimpanzee greeting another may poke out its lips in what looks like a kissing action (**1**, overleaf).

- A subordinate chimpanzee lowers itself when it meets one of superior status, much as a human subject might bow or kneel to a monarch.

HUMANS AND THE PRIMATE INHERITANCE
For us, though, nonvocal communication has been replaced (through evolution) by something far more effective – speech. Nonverbal communication remains, however,

- to reinforce and complement spoken statements;

- to replace spoken statements if, for example, secrecy is required or distance prevents effective verbal communication;

- as a means of expressing feeling and opinion, both consciously and subconsciously;

- as a means of greeting, and displaying status and relationship ties; and

- as a means of delivering insults.

THE FACE AND FORELIMBS

Human potential for posturing and gesturing owes much to the way in which evolutionary changes resulted in a redesigned face and forelimbs. These are important because facial expressions and gesticulations are the main components of body language.

THE ANIMAL FACE

Fish, reptiles and primitive mammals, such as the opossum, demonstrate little in the way of facial expression. They stare and, at most, gape when threatened. More advanced mammals, such as cats, are able to move the ears, eyes and mouth to signal basic moods – fear and hostility, for instance (**1**). Primates (especially monkeys, apes and humans) have the most mobile faces of all.

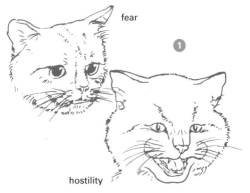

fear

1

hostility

THE PRIMATE FACE

The primate face expresses feelings such as fear, friendliness and hostility. By studying apes and monkeys, researchers have shown that basic human facial expressions (see pp. 26–32) are part of a more general primate inheritance. Like humans, apes and monkeys will:

- scowl if angry (**1**);
- snarl with rage, showing the front teeth (**2**);
- raise the eyebrows if frightened (**3**);
- pull the corners of the mouth right back if terrified, opening the mouth wide enough to show the molar teeth (**4**), and scream.

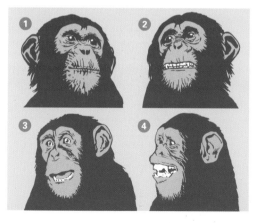

Animal forelimbs
All animal forelimbs evolved from the muscular lobed
pectoral fins of certain prehistoric fish. Some mammals'
forelimbs evolved as paws and hooves, which can be used
expressively. An excited horse, for example, will stamp or
paw the ground; these are, however, the only gestures it
can make with its forelimbs.

Primate forelimbs
Power grip Primates' forelimbs evolved as arms and
flexible hands with thumbs and fingers able to grasp
branches and seize food in a good 'power grip' (**1**), as
their owners climbed or swung from tree to tree. Not all
primates, however, have fine 'precision grips' which enable
them to manipulate smaller objects precisely.

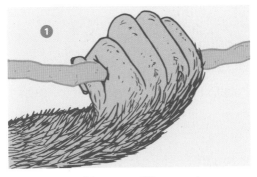

Precision grip in chimpanzees Chimpanzees have a
comparatively highly developed precision grip (**2**, overleaf)

and so are able to manufacture and use a simple tool. They break off and strip twigs to go poking in termite hills (**3**) for termites, which they eat.